ONE-DAY
GETAWAYS

from Vancouver

ONE-DAY
GETAWAYS
from Vancouver

Jack Christie

GREYSTONE BOOKS
Douglas & McIntyre
Vancouver/Toronto

Greystone Books
A division of Douglas & McIntyre Ltd.
1615 Venables Street
Vancouver, British Columbia V5L 2H1

Canadian Cataloguing in Publication Data

Christie, Jack, 1946-
    One-day getaways from Vancouver

    "Greystone Books."
    ISBN 1-55054-103-X

    1. British Columbia—Tours. I. Title.
FC3817.4.C47 1994   917.11'3044   C94-910088-9
F1087.C47 1994

Photos by Louise Christie
Maps by Kelly Alm
Edited by Maja Grip
Typeset by Vancouver Desktop Publishing Centre
Printed and bound in Canada

To my soulmate Louise, to my mentor Doug McKee, and to my schoolmate Scott King. Life has blessed me with untarnishable memories of good times shared together.

CONTENTS

FRASER RIVER ESTUARY

THE GULF ISLANDS

FOREWORD

Since my first book, *Day Trips from Vancouver*, appeared in June 1989, my wife and sons and I have continued to uncover more outdoor destinations, recording our experiences in words and photographs. *Day Trips* is now in its fifth printing, and there are no signs that the interest—or the topic—has been exhausted.

A B.C. Parks visitor survey carried out by the provincial government reveals an interesting profile of day trippers in the 1990s. Ninety-five percent said their park visit met or exceeded their expectations. On average, the group size was four people, their visit lasted five hours, they travelled 96 kilometres to the park, and they spent $57 on the day of their trip. This is my audience. These are my kind of people.

Much like you, I'm constantly amazed at how my expectations are exceeded every time I venture outdoors. This is one of the many positive rewards awaiting day trippers with even the mildest of ambitions. In preparing *One-day Getaways* my challenge has been to find ways to convey this sense of fulfilment, coloured with surprise and awe, seasoned by experience.

Where *Day Trips* cast a wide net, *One-day Getaways* takes a much closer look at destinations nearer Vancouver, including Howe Sound, the North Shore, Richmond, Surrey, Ladner, Langley, Matsqui and the Dewdney-Alouette region, with an emphasis on where to find quiet time in a natural setting only a short distance from the noise and the hurry of the city. More distant locales are included, too, such as the southern Gulf Islands; experience will quickly demonstrate to the reader that this is a distance born of perception rather than fact. All of the new destinations highlighted here are quickly attainable, whether you plan your trip far in advance or head out on the spur of the moment. (And yes, I do include camping information for those times when you'd like to extend your visit overnight.)

Many of the pioneer trails and buildings I have encountered won't be here much longer. I write for Lower Mainland residents and visitors who wish to catch a glimpse of this rich but quickly vanishing past before it has been subdivided into oblivion. Even as our heritage disappears, though, new parks and trails are being set aside each year, and *One-day Getaways* maps them out for you. All levels of government are following the public lead more closely when deciding where to create new parkland, and I give my readers every encouragement to exploit this trend. We still have a chance to preserve more than just a memory of our heritage if we get out there and see it for ourselves.

* * *

Where reading a book is most often a solitary and individual experience, writing one requires a group effort. As always, thanks go to my family for faithfully answering the bell when the time came for another round of research. Often we visit a place on a whim, only to find ourselves drawn back time and again for more research and photographs. Louise, Athal and Arrlann, Bob and Jackie — all are the best company and most patient models an outdoors writer could wish for.

Appreciation for constant encouragement and positive suggestions goes to Charles Campbell, Naomi Pauls, Lianne Heller and Martin Dunphy at the *Georgia Straight*. Thanks also to Dan McLeod and the entire staff.

The photographic advice and service from Bob and James Abbott and Margaret Jorstead at Action Reprographics has been of great value to us in preparing this book.

Bryan Swan, Chris O'Hagan and Ernie Millar at Conti Computer Systems provided help above and beyond the call of customer service.

I'm blessed to have had Maja Grip to streamline the flow of words with her editing expertise, Kelly Alm to craft the maps and Greystone Books' Terri Wershler and Rob Sanders to guide the overall production.

The works of Maggie Paquet, Randy Stoltmann, Peggy Ward, Roger and Ethel Freeman, David and Mary Macaree, Bruce Obee, Elaine Jones, Mary and Ted Bentley, Peter Murray and Roger Tory Peterson have all been helpful.

Finally, thanks to the producers and staff at CBC-Radio and BCTV for the air time, to the staff at Isadora's for providing spare time and to all those listeners and readers who offer advice, suggestions and constant encouragement.

LIST OF MAPS

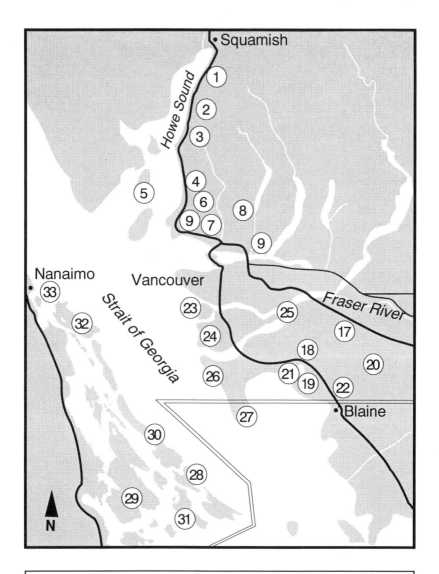

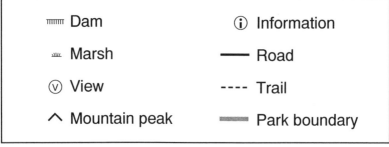

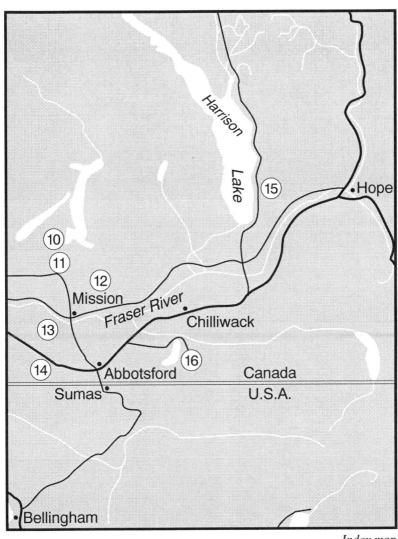

Index map

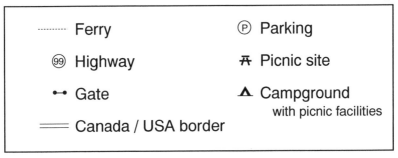

⋯⋯⋯ Ferry		℗ Parking	
⑨⑨ Highway		🎋 Picnic site	
•–• Gate		⛺ Campground	
══ Canada / USA border		with picnic facilities	

HOWE SOUND |

STEEP SLOPES
AND CLEAR CREEKS

Howe Sound without water would be an interesting sight, its topography telling the tale of the most recent glacial period. Smack in the middle of the sound off the shores of Porteau Cove is a steep ridge, running in a north-south direction, that was pushed up by the forward edge of ice. The ridge marks the limit of the glacier's advance.

The extremely steep mountainsides that rise above Howe Sound are some of the most rugged in the world—certainly in the Coast Mountains, as anyone who has ventured into the country behind the North Shore can testify. Howe Sound's Britannia Range is a leaf from a thicker textbook of peaks that run east to Golden Ears park. Owing to the sheerness of the land, runoff rushes down the creekbeds in torrents and the slopes of Howe Sound stream with white. Disbrow, Montizambert, Charles, Newman, Lone Tree, Harvey, Alberta, Magnesia— the litany of creeks feeding into Howe Sound goes on and on.

Without question the primary outdoor pursuit around the sound is sightseeing by car, closely followed by hiking. As the water link of the Sea-to-Sky Highway, Howe Sound is a major player in the big, picturesque scene laid out before you on the way to Squamish and Whistler. No other setting can compete when the sound captures rays of light from the setting sun on its flat calm expanse, or match the view from its shoreline as the early morning sun torches peaks in the Tantalus Range.

Here are some of the features you'll pass or cross as you drive along Howe Sound from Horseshoe Bay (kilometre 0) to Squamish (kilometre 44): Sunset Marina (km 5); Sclufield Creek (km

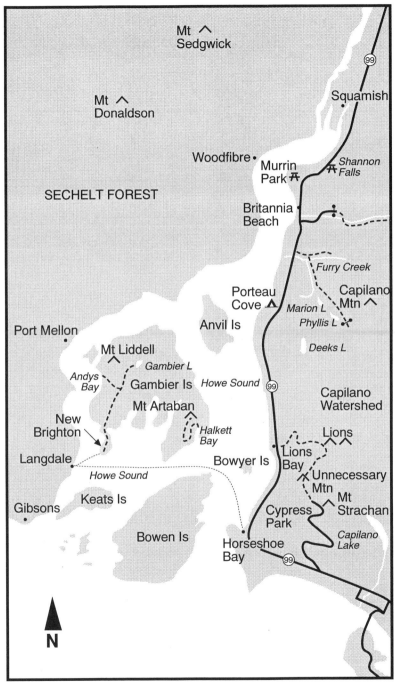

Mt Sedgwick

Mt Donaldson

SECHELT FOREST

Woodfibre

Murrin Park

Shannon Falls

Squamish

99

Britannia Beach

Furry Creek

Porteau Cove

Capilano Mtn

Marion L

Phyllis L

Anvil Is

Port Mellon

Deeks L

Mt Liddell

Gambier L

Andys Bay

Gambier Is

Howe Sound

99

Capilano Watershed

Mt Artaban

New Brighton

Halkett Bay

Lions

Langdale

Howe Sound

Bowyer Is

Lions Bay

Unnecessary Mtn

Gibsons

Keats Is

Cypress Park

Mt Strachan

Bowen Is

Horseshoe Bay

Capilano Lake

99

N

Howe Sound

3

Leaving Horseshoe Bay

5.1); Montizambert Creek (km 5.6); Strip Creek (km 6.8); Charles Creek (km 7.3); Turpin Creek (km 7.7); Newman Creek (km 8.5); Lone Tree Creek (km 9.8); Lions Bay (km 11); Rundle Creek (km 11.2); Harvey Creek (km 11.7); Alberta Creek (km 12); Magnesia Creek (km 13.5); M (Yahoo) Creek (km 14); a rest area at km 15; Loggers Creek (km 16.7); Deeks Creek (km 17.3); Pacific Great Eastern roadside plaque (km 20); Brunswick Creek (km 20.4); Bertram Creek (km 21.6); Deeks Creek (km 22); Howe Sound Crest trailhead (km 23); Porteau Cove Provincial Park (km 24); Furry Creek (km 27); Daisy Creek (km 31); Thistle Creek (km 31.5); Britannia Creek (km 33); Murrin Provincial Park (km 35.7); Petgill Lake trailhead (km 36.5); Gonzalez Creek (km 38.5); Shannon Falls Provincial Park (km 40.5); Stawamus River (km 42.5). Whew.

Leave your car and climb just a short distance: in late summer and fall you can see where the turquoise waters of the glacier-fed Squamish River blend with the deep blue of Howe Sound. Earlier in the year, when mineral particles in the river water are coarser, the Squamish outflow is closer to pea soup in hue.

If you want a front-row seat any time of year, try one of the getaways I've selected from Howe Sound's repertoire. Joining you will be seals and eagles, otters and bears, geese and deer, who love Howe Sound as much as we do.

1 | BRITANNIA BEACH

CLIMBING ◀
FISHING ◀
HIKING ◀
HISTORIC SITES ◀
PICNICKING ◀
SIGHTSEEING ◀
WALKING ◀

Depending on the time of year, you can stop at Britannia Beach (21 mi./34 km north of Horseshoe Bay) for a quick warmup while on your way north along the Sea-to-Sky Highway, use it as a rendezvous point for meeting friends, explore the B.C. Museum of Mining, walk over to a former settlement at nearby Minaty Bay or do some serious exploring in the surrounding back country where Sky Pilot Mountain predominates.

After a lull of two decades—the years between the closing of the local mine and the opening of the Coast Mountain Circle Route—Britannia Beach is regaining its popularity as the little village finds colourful ways to dress itself up. Today there's Jane's Coffeehouse Gallery, a tea room and craft shop, to complement the Ninety-Niner Restaurant, a fixture at Britannia Beach since the road was first paved.

One reason for this increased attention is Britannia Beach's historic appeal. Another is that the 350 Britannia residents refuse to say die and instead continue beautifying their boulder-strewn landscape. Perhaps as compensation, nature has provided the village with a scenic vista unparallelled on Howe Sound. Now if it only had a sandy beach!

There are few places in the Lower Mainland whose history is as nakedly exposed as at Britannia Beach. Copper mining began here in the early 1900s and was the engine driving the town's economy until the last shift came out of the mining shafts in 1979—an impressive run by any mining standards.

The settlement of Britannia Beach predated the establishment of the mine by some 40 years. A prospector named it after the mountain range rising behind the town. In turn, Captain Richards, commander of the Royal Navy survey ship *Plumper*, had named the range after the English naval vessel *Britannia*, which had seen distinguished service in several battles in the late 18th and early 19th centuries (the ship never actually sailed in B.C. waters).

A plaque mounted in Britannia Beach Memorial Park describes in detail how the mine started operation in 1905. When an expanded ore concentrator was constructed in 1912 the mine became a significant operation. With a workforce of over 1000, Britannia Mines became one of Canada's largest during the 1920s and 1930s.

Over the course of the mine's operating history 60,000 people called Britannia Beach home. Many still return periodically to see what's left of their community. Little remains now except a smattering of company buildings and a mixture of homes, some well kept, some abandoned, tucked into the hillside above the beach.

The size and number of pilings beneath Britannia's wharf attest to the scale of activity that was carried on in the town's glory years. A former cruise ship, the *Prince George*, has been moored here for several years now. The ship last saw service as a workers' residence in Alaska, during the cleanup operation following the *Exxon Valdez* oil spill. For now, like the concentrate mill attached to the hillside on the opposite side of the highway, the *Prince George* is idle. It would cost as much to scrap either as it would to restore them, so for now they sit in limbo.

Mild-mannered Britannia Creek runs through the middle of the village, following a trench that channels through an obvious flood plain and out under a cheerily painted orange metal bridge to the ocean. Life in Britannia isn't always this carefree. In 1991, creek waters rampaged at the urging of a ferocious rainstorm that began on August 29 and continued for four days. So violent was the action of water in Britannia Creek that it forced closure of Highway 99 and almost took out the village itself. Only through valiant effort did residents manage to keep the waters at bay and rescue most of their homes. Today, much of the area around the creek still has the appearance of a rocky flood plain. Boulders in the creek itself show signs of acid rock drainage, a condition where heavy metals contained in extracted ores begin to dissolve when exposed to the air.

Sky Pilot Mountain, seen from the old Mount Sheer minesite

During summer months the B.C. Museum of Mining, a national historic site, offers guided tours through the old mine. Each year it adds another memento to its collection. This includes a giant 235-ton Electric Haulpack truck, transferred to Britannia Beach museum from the copper-mine site at Logan Lake, south of Kamloops. In its 12 years of service the truck carried 30 million tonnes of copper ore and thus earned this special resting place. Even if you're not in the mood for a look underground, stop in at the museum's headquarters, where archival photographs are on view along with showcases of mineral samples and mining memorabilia. There's also a gift shop where related items are available for purchase.

MOUNT SHEER MINE SITE   A road runs through the town and back up into the folds of the Britannia Range, to the sides of aptly named Mount Sheer. Along the way it passes another mine shaft. The easy 3-mi. (4.5-km) walk to the old site, abandoned in 1958, follows the original road, a 90-minute journey one way.

To reach the gate where the trail begins, turn in at the entrance to the B.C. Museum of Mining, drive past the mining offices, and continue nearly a mile (1.4 km) uphill on the paved road, bearing right at all times. There's plenty of room for parking on the street in front of the gate.

As you begin to walk uphill, you pass the water supply station for the town, and then in 10 minutes the town dump. You may see a bear or two around the dump, on your way up or down—give them a wide berth. (When exploring anywhere in the back country you will come across signs of bears, particularly during berry season. Upcoming hibernation is the motivating force behind bear activity; during their waking months they must feed constantly, storing up fat to carry them through their sleepy time.)

The old road narrows to little more than a comfortably wide trail as it climbs towards the Mount Sheer mine site. Watch for a fork in the road after you've been walking for about an hour. Follow uphill to the right to reach the abandoned mine, 30 minutes away.

At the clearing around the Mount Sheer mine, racks in old sheds still hold core samples. The sole of a boot, a battered kettle and a concrete footprint or two are signs of the former occupants. The entrance to the old mine shaft is barricaded to prevent entry, though it seems some have tried to force a way in despite the warning signs.

What is most pleasant about this location is the open view to the north and east. The lofty pinnacle of Sky Pilot Mountain is most prominent. Mount Sheer and the profile of Goat Ridge rise on either side of it. From here you get an excellent close-up of the range only hinted at from Highway 99. Utopia Lake, the headwaters of Britannia Creek, lies hidden in the slopes between Mount Sheer and Sky Pilot Mountain.

The walk to the mine site is a easy uphill jaunt, good for a half-day exploration. Any farther and you're in for an extended workout along a poorly marked route. (A good approach to exploring Sky Pilot Mountain is to join a group such as the Alpine Club of Canada, which regularly schedules outings in this region. Phone 983-9802.)

MURRIN PROVINCIAL PARK   This small park lies about 2 mi. (3 km) north of Britannia Beach on the west side of Highway 99. It's hard to miss: the waters of Browning Lake, the park's most prominent feature, practically lap the shoulder of the highway. Picnic tables are positioned around the lake's west side, some in direct sunlight, others in partial shade. You'll almost always see someone fishing here as the lake is well stocked with rainbow trout. For years popular lore held that fishing in Browning Lake was restricted to the younger, 14-and-under crowd; actually, all anyone needs is a valid fishing licence to enjoy throwing in a line.

Steep but easily accessible cliffs rise on the west and north sides of the 60-acre (24-ha) park, making it a popular destination for rockclimbers who wish to work on their technique.

Across the highway from the parking lot and just north is the entrance to a favourite Howe Sound hiking trail to nearby Petgill Lake, a 7-mi. (11-km) round trip that will take between five and six hours to complete. Everything you need to know is posted on the little kiosk at trailhead. You don't need to go the full distance in order to enjoy the scenic viewpoints from this well-marked trail. Just surmount the first steep pitch and Howe Sound will be laid out before your eyes. The higher you go (total elevation gain is only 1968 ft./600 m), the better the views of the mountains to the east and north, including Sky Pilot and Garibaldi.

2 | FURRY CREEK

Care for a walk in the woods by a mountain stream to a hidden lake? That's what a visit to Furry Creek is all about, as straightforward as a golf ball hit well off one of the tees on the Furry Creek course, which you pass beside for starters.

As you drive along Highway 99 between Horseshoe Bay and Squamish, you cross more than a dozen creeks that flow down off the mountainside into Howe Sound. Most of these run through narrow gorges carved into the rock face before spilling into the ocean. From the car the most you can hope for is a quick glimpse of their shaded wet passageways. My imagination finds these places inviting, especially on hot sunny days, but also after storms when the creeks are high and waterfalls are pouring forth their contents. Don't underestimate their power: in years past they have brought with them highway delays and closures, fierce destruction and sometimes death. This stretch of Highway 99 is not to be trifled with during times of heavy rainfall. Still, nature's most extreme manifestations can be most enthralling, like the fireworks allure of a volcano erupting, or the chance to see the invisible face of the wind revealed as it whips seafoam off the curling waves of surf.

Along Howe Sound, there are several places where you can park and within a few minutes walk up beside a creek. Furry Creek, together with Shannon Falls and Britannia Beach, is one of the more accessible ones. Oliver Furry was a trapper and prospector who staked claims around Britannia Creek, which led the way to the development of rich copper mines in the vicinity. A look at a survey map of the area reveals a pattern of hundreds of claims, laid out like residential lots in a housing development.

Copper's reign ended in the late 1970s, and today Furry Creek is undergoing a radical change. The golf course built by the Tanas Corporation carpets the slopes on each side of the highway. The boulder-filled creekbed cuts down through the middle of an ambitious project that will eventually see luxurious homes ringing the course. This development will soon unmask what was once an anonymous road leading uphill beside the creek through a second-growth forest. At present, the area is in the midst of full-tilt construction. For the moment, Furry Creek is best approached during the lull of off-duty hours when the road is free of big trucks. (A new approach to Marion and Phyllis lakes, originating from Porteau Cove, was roughed out by members of the North Shore Hikers in late 1993.)

As you travel north on Highway 99, 2 mi. (3 km) past Porteau Cove, watch for a side road to the east of the highway as soon as you cross the bridge over Furry Creek. There is a yellow gate here and signs warning "No Trespassing" (specifically intended to keep out vehicles). You must walk from here. There is room enough for a half-dozen cars to park on the shoulder beside the gate, more space on the opposite side of the highway, and more slightly uphill, where there is a wide paved shoulder. Be careful crossing the road on foot.

Soon after you begin up the road beyond the gate, watch for a metal trail marker affixed to the trunk of an old Douglas fir—it informs anyone with eyes sharp enough to spot it that this trail, maintained by the North Shore Hikers, leads to Beth Lake. Another such marker appears on a tree beside the bridge across Furry Creek in 30 minutes' time.

Beth Lake is one of several small pools held in the folds of the surrounding mountains. Phyllis and Marion lakes are two others. Although the trail to Beth Lake has fallen into disuse—in part, I suspect, because the areas above its shore are not as pretty now that logging has cleared large sections at higher elevations—it does offer views of Capilano Mountain's permanent snowcap. (Check with the North Shore Hikers as to its status with their organization. Phone 925-9312.)

The slopes surrounding Phyllis and Marion lakes remain relatively unscathed, brushed out only where tall hydro pylons support cables carrying power to Vancouver. The clearing

Log bridge over Furry Creek

around these is relatively minor compared to the broad, empty swaths left by logging. A service road leads to the lakes, providing a clear approach that will give your legs a good workout without putting them to the ultimate fitness test presented by trails such as the one leading to the Lions.

From the outset, it's obvious that as you climb the road you are entering into the folds of the surrounding mountains. These hillsides are steep, and some of the new homes will have precarious perches indeed. It will take you 20 minutes to reach the first major divide in the road; stay to the right and head towards the sound of Furry Creek, which is beginning to reveal itself at the bottom of the steep slope beside the road. Good views of Howe Sound accompany the road as it rises above the golf course. After a little more than 30 minutes you reach the new "old" bridge over Furry Creek. Although its thick timbers look as if they've been in place for decades, it was actually put in place only in 1993 to replace one that had been washed out.

In the creekbed above the bridge is a well-balanced staircase of boulders through which Furry Creek makes its descent. In the backwaters of the creek are clear pools. It's actually quite a scramble to get down to the creekbed from the bridge, should you wish to try. From the bridge, it's clear that two narrow valleys converge here. Out of sight and just downstream from the bridge, the waters of Phyllis Creek blend with those of Furry. Even at Furry's lowest water levels, the voice of the creek drowns out everything else. When it's at its highest pitch you can hear boulders being shifted around by the force of the flow.

To the left of the bridge, an old road follows Furry Creek uphill on its north side. A new fence prevents vehicular traffic from proceeding, though the very condition of the road itself seems prohibitive enough. It's worth a walk up this road to see the remnants of an old cement catch-basin that once held back debris. Tanas dynamited it in 1992 to the applause of local environmental officials, who cheered to see the creek allowed to assume its original nature. The road ends here. In the forest on its north side there are still signs of the small-scale mining activity that was pursued until quite recently.

Crossing the Furry Creek bridge puts you on the road to Marion and Phyllis lakes, a distance you can probably cover in less than 90 minutes. No one I've ever met on this road has been in a hurry. (In fact, you're unlikely to meet anyone on the road, period.) If you don't want to go all the way to the lakes, but are up here just for a preliminary look-around, at least cross the Furry Creek bridge and walk uphill a short distance to the next bridge, which crosses Phyllis Creek, if only for the sake of comparison. The creekbed here has a boulder garden of its own, though on a somewhat steeper and more modest scale than that of Furry.

The road climbs uphill past the bridge at a moderate rate, shaded by the overhanging branches of a climax forest of alder and the occasional maple. On the forest floor beneath them young hemlock advance upward with each passing year; it will be their turn to take over when the alder begin to drop.

Enjoy the shade as you climb. You soon reach the first hydro pylon, where the road becomes more open. From here the views are all to the northwest and are of the glaciated broad southern flanks of the Tantalus Range. Below, mostly hidden to the north, is Phyllis Creek.

A half-hour from where you first crossed Phyllis Creek is a second bridge. The creek is broader and shallower here. Along the way the road branches in several places; stay on the well-worn, better-used sections in each case. You may rightly sense as you walk south along the road that you are in fact headed straight towards Vancouver. In the distance, through a gap in the mountains, you can see nothing but the open sky above the Fraser River estuary. Rising unseen on the left is Capilano Mountain; only rarely will you catch sight of the shoulders of Mount Windsor or Deeks Peak on your right.

In another 30 minutes, after a stretch of road that lends itself to the sort of quiet contemplation that frequently occurs when there isn't that much new to see as you walk, you will find yourself beside Marion Lake, albeit on the road above its shoreline. Getting to lakeside is tricky. Watch carefully for a steep descent at the lake's northern end. There aren't many good approaches on Marion Lake's shoreline even after you've made the descent, as it is either quite rocky or marshy. Better to keep walking for another 10 minutes to reach Phyllis Lake, though the access here is only marginally better than at Marion.

Before you actually reach Phyllis you may glimpse its waters through the open forest. On a sunny day, the first hint of its presence will be the shimmer of light on its surface. The road descends towards the lake but never leads directly to the shoreline. Instead, you'll have to watch for an open approach beside a culvert where old tree trunks and boulders form an intricate and steep, jigsaw trail. If you are able, climb down here onto a rocky outcrop beside the lake and you will have an open place on which to picnic, sunbathe and perhaps dive into the cool waters of Phyllis Lake. Small fish jump for insects, hinting at larger brethren in the deeper sections of the lake. Discarded lures, weights and nylon line on the rocks indicate that others have tried their luck here. Perhaps this detritus is also a sign of their frustration.

Phyllis Lake is larger than it first appears. Its shoreline curves south out of view from this rock pad. You can swim out to the middle of the lake to see the full extent of its size, or else walk to its southern end, where the road suddenly meets an imposing metal fence demarcating the border of Vancouver's watershed. Entrance is quite obviously restricted past here. Turn back to the hush of the lake, leaving the crackling of the hydro wires behind. Experience once again the quiet of the little lake, with its fat lily pads and surrounding slopes of elegant old-growth forest. Take your time as you return down the road that brought you here from Furry Creek. This is a visit to share with friends who are looking for some exercise and fresh air, one that will allow a companionable ebb and flow in conversation as the day passes—an accomplishment in itself.

3 | PORTEAU COVE PROVINCIAL PARK

BOATING ◄
CAMPING ◄
DIVING ◄
PADDLING ◄
PICNICKING ◄
SWIMMING ◄

For all of its beauty, Howe Sound provides few points of public access along its rugged shoreline. In most places the mountains plunge sharply into the waters of the deep fiord (Canada's most southerly), forcing the railroad and the highway close together, with scant room left over for visitors to spread a picnic blanket, let alone set up a tent. One of the few places where these things *are* possible is Porteau Cove Provincial Park.

There was once a small settlement in the sheltered bay. Little remains except the formal stone wall around the cove's hidden west side. In fact, from the road it is almost impossible to see the cove that is one of this park's most attractive features. Instead, as you travel Highway 99, the beach and jetty are what catch the eye. Only in winter, once the leaves are down, is it possible to see through the surrounding forest into the little cove itself.

As you turn into the park, located 15.5 mi. (25 km) north of Horseshoe Bay (twice that from Vancouver), you pass information signs, directed at divers, that detail the location of several marine vessels scuttled offshore specifically for underwater exploration. The first of these boats was sunk in 1981 when the park was opened. Marine life is attracted to such wrecks, making a dive even more exciting. For this reason the signs also warn visitors that fishing is not permitted within the park. Watching divers hardly qualifies as spectator sport. But that said, there is something rather entertaining about a group of rubber-clad people entering or emerging from the cold waters of the sound while you enjoy your picnic at one of the numerous tables

16

Anvil Island from Porteau Cove lookout

spread around the broad, driftwood-littered beaches on both sides of the jetty. Small floats positioned offshore help divers orient themselves. Divers affix a flag to the top of these if they are diving below, warning boaters to stay well away. Porteau Cove is also a designated provincial marine park with sheltered moorage.

(In the past several years the provincial government has upgraded the docking facilities so that they may be used by a ferry in case of emergency. This is in response to numerous closures of Highway 99 due to rockfalls, one of which blocked the road for over a week and stranded many motorists on their way south from Whistler. The opening of the Duffey Lake Road has provided another alternative route.)

If you are visiting Porteau for the day, you can use the large parking area beside the jetty. This is a wonderful place to take a break from highway traffic and enjoy the spectacular views of Howe Sound, with Anvil Island's obvious profile to the southwest and the peaks of the Tantalus Range rising in the northwest. The gravel beach slopes gently into the sound. On days when the tide is low and the sun high, the gravel heats up and warms the incoming waters, making swimming here a pleasure.

This is the only provincial park on the sound accessible by

car, so the 59 campsites are in constant use (15 are walk-in sites). Even if you are visiting just for the day, have a look at Porteau's camping facilities with an eye to making plans for a future visit. If you head here with the intention of staying overnight, arrive early and have a contingency plan in case all the spaces have been taken. (A sign posted in front of the small gatehouse will tell you if anything is available.) The drive-in sites go quickly throughout the summer and on Friday and Saturday nights from May to October, but there is usually a good chance of getting one of the walk-in sites even if you arrive late, except in the months of June to August. A user fee is collected from April to October: about $15 for drive-in sites and half that for walk-ins.

As soon as you enter the campground, bear right to see if any of the oceanfront sites are vacant. In the middle of the campground is a washroom facility complete with showers.

The walk-in sites are located at the far end of the campground road. From the walk-in parking lot to the sites is only a short distance, easily covered in several minutes. An amphitheatre is located between the drive-in and walk-in campsites. Interpretive displays are presented here at one of the most scenic locations in the park on summer evenings.

Because there is so little level land, most sites are relatively closely spaced compared to other provincial parks. Campsite 44, at the westernmost end of the road next to the walk-in parking, is one of the few that have some breathing room. It sits in the shelter of the Sitka spruce forest and commands an attractive view of the sound. The only drawback is its proximity to the railroad tracks. Visitors can count on several trains passing by at all hours of day or night, including the dayliner service to Prince George, a pretty sight of sinewy silver as it heads north around 8:15 in the morning and south at 7:45 at night. The dayliner glides by, but the heavily loaded freight trains, pulled and pushed by four drumming diesel locomotives, create an entirely different soundscape. Parents should warn young children that they may hear these behemoths in the night, so they won't worry that their world is suddenly coming to an end.

Discreetly tucked in behind the walk-in sites is the cove itself. An open lawn is laid out beside the cove, a small bridge spanning the narrow backwater. A service road leads west to the park caretaker's residence (at present the public cannot explore any farther than here).

Take a walk to the viewpoint on the trail that leads west from the walk-in sites and up onto the forested bluff. Stunted shore pines (a coastal variety of lodgepole pine) and stately Sitka spruce provide shelter on the point, from where you can look down on the cove or out across the waters of the sound. This is a quiet place in which to enjoy the surroundings, especially in the early or late hours of the day, or to stop for an off-season breather from the highway.

The public boat launch at Porteau Cove is the only one accessible from Highway 99 between Horseshoe Bay and Squamish. There are often times when Howe Sound is flat calm, a perfect invitation to enjoy a paddle; however, always be aware that strong winds can rise quickly. Sticking close to shore you can safely enjoy views of the Howe Sound Crest and Britannia ranges that are not otherwise revealed from land. If you paddle north to Furry Creek, look for pictographs painted on the rock face on the north side of the small bay just past the creek's entrance into Howe Sound.

4 | THE LIONS

Let's not mince words: this is a hike, pure and simple. Not a warmup hike either, but a real test of what kind of shape your body's in. As a reward for making this supreme effort you will have the finest viewpoint imaginable to offset the muscle aches you'll probably experience for several days afterwards.

These two prominent peaks, the Lions (known as the Sisters by local native people, and as Sheba's Paps by some turn-of-the-century Europeans) are as much a part of our skyline as the suspension bridge named after them which links Vancouver to the North Shore. They appear both distant and near, simultaneously.

One approach is along the Howe Sound Crest trail that leads north from Cypress Bowl Provincial Park, but be warned: even if you're in good condition it will take plenty of time, effort and patience to reach them by this route. Patience is the ingredient most required when, after several hours of up-and-downing, with hardly a viewpoint to justify the effort, you must cross Unnecessary Mountain to reach the ridge beside the two crumbling spires. Unnecessary Mountain is no small or joking matter, requiring considerable exertion to surmount on a route that has never received the care and attention that trail builders have shown on other North Shore trails, including the alternate route to the Lions that begins from Lions Bay.

When you compare the two approaches, the decision comes down to a trade-off between the time required for crossing on the Howe Sound Crest and the steepness of the Lions Bay route. The choice is yours. My recommendation is to wait for a warm

20

(not hot) day in late summer or early fall and climb to the Lions on the trail that leads above Lions Bay.

You'll get a good look at the west Lion if you look up from Highway 99 as you pass through Lions Bay, 7 mi. (11 km) north of Horseshoe Bay, where the highway crosses the bridge over Harvey Creek. Its size makes it seem closer than it actually is. Unless you're one of the triathletes who regularly run up and down the Lions route in under four hours as part of their training program, plan to take four hours to climb one way from the trailhead in Lions Bay to the ridge below the west Lion. You should be in good shape before you attempt to go the entire distance. This is a hike for the end of a summer when your legs have been tested by lesser climbs elsewhere, a "gold-medal hike" to do as a reward or provide a climax to the season.

The later in the year you undertake this climb, the better the views from lower elevations as you make the ascent. Much of the forest that lines the old road for the first hour of your hike is deciduous. Broad-leaf maple provides shade earlier in the summer, rich hues of colour in September and then, with the downing of its leaves, an open view of Howe Sound in October and November. Snow will probably impede your passage at higher elevations from then through June or July. A few patches of snow on the sheltered north flank of the west Lion rarely melt from one year to the next.

Finding your way to the trailhead is one of the little challenges. Take the second entrance to Lions Bay from Highway 99 (Oceanview) as you travel north from Horseshoe Bay. Follow the signs pointing left towards the convenience store. Turn right on Centre, left on Bayview, left on Mountain Drive and finally left again on Sunset. As you climb through the neighbourhood you'll pass the elementary school, next to which is a parking lot. If you arrive at the trailhead and find that all parking spaces there have been taken, you can park at this overflow lot, but before descending back to the school check to see if there is any space on Sunset south of Mountain Drive. If there is (the parking restrictions are well marked), you will save yourself an extra 10 minutes climbing uphill—and believe me, you'll need to conserve all of the resources you've brought with you to accomplish this hike.

However, you don't have to cover the entire route in order to experience many of the extraordinary features it has to offer.

Viewpoints appear at intervals for the first hour as the wide trail (a fire road) winds its way uphill through a series of switchbacks. As you round the corner at each turn another long stretch of road confronts you. Early on the road divides, with the left blocked by a fence and a warning sign to keep out. After 30 minutes a view of Howe Sound opens up when the leaves are down. After 40 minutes the trail divides again; an arrow fashioned out of stones points the way. You will encounter several of these stone arrows in the first 90 minutes, after which orange and silver metal markers affixed to the sides of trees take over. This is not a hard trail to follow. Much of the credit for trail maintenance goes to the B.C. Mountaineer Club, which has adopted the Lions trail.

You come to the first major viewpoint after you have been on the trail for an hour. Looking south from the top of a debris chute you can easily identify Horseshoe Bay and modest-sized Bowyer Island offshore in Howe Sound. The fire road begins to narrow and is replaced by a well-kept trail. A view of Lions Bay far below occurs just after the trail crosses in front of a rock face beside which a small creek flows. As you walk along, the trail blends with a rocky creekbed, passes another stone arrow and signpost, then begins to descend towards Harvey Creek, which you can hear in the distance. Along the way now are several lovely big old Douglas fir trees on the steep slope bordering the trail.

Ninety minutes after starting out you'll be thankful for the efforts of the Mountaineers, who have installed rudimentary wooden steps where the trail approaches Harvey Creek. The best time to cross the creek is in fall, when it's at its lowest point; during rainy spells, crossing the rampaging waters can be perilous. The boulders in the creek are popular spots on which to sunbathe and gather your breath for the climb ahead. Harvey Creek forces an opening in the canopy of tree branches. If you've been feeling closed in, here is the place to enjoy some sky. The creek provides water for the Lions Bay community, so please be extremely careful not to pollute it in any way.

As the trail climbs into the forest above Harvey Creek, one of the first real surprises for visitors will be the appearance of substantial old-growth forest. When you enter a large clearing with an old fire-ring, bear left to pick up the trail.

After you leave Harvey Creek, experience the hush of the

The west Lion

Overlooking Lions Bay, southwest from the base of the Lions

forest as you climb steadily uphill for the next 30 minutes. A
good resting place occurs at a viewpoint where there are smooth
boulders for seats and sunshine for warmth. Several minutes
later you reach one of the most gorgeous spots on the mountainside. A beautifully spaced grove of ramrod-straight balsam
fir tower above, while a newer forest of western hemlock below
have a uniform integrity of their own. Ten minutes into this
stand of fir brings you to the best viewpoint yet of Howe Sound.
Now all of Gambier island is revealed, as is the nest of smaller
islands west of Bowen, and across to the Sunshine Coast.

By the time you've been on the trail for a little over three
hours (breaks included) you'll be ready for the experience of
seeing the west Lion nearby as you reach a clearing above the
forest. At this point you may well have begun to experience a
sense of giddy euphoria. It might as well be Machu Picchu that
rises before your eyes. You've made it, and the Lions are now
close enough to taste. All you need to worry about is saving
enough strength in your legs and enough daylight in the sky
for your trip down. (By the time you've made your descent back
to this point, your knees may be wobbling as if you'd just
downed a triple shot of tequila.)

Keeping all this in mind, head up towards the nearby ridge.

(Stash anything unwanted before the final ascent.) More than at any other time on the climb you'll want to be wearing sturdy boots with a stiff sole. Footing becomes trickier as you hop from boulder to boulder up the last incline to the ridge. Once you're on the ridge a better path establishes itself and you can walk more leisurely. Find yourself a seat on one of the numerous plateaus, or feast on this view of a lifetime: the landscape stretches off into fabulous oblivion on all sides. In late summer the narrow gullies are filled with a low ground cover of heather, turning a burnt red, and a companion bush on whose stems are hanging blueberries, moist and tart—perfect for the thirst you developed climbing that last stretch.

Seldom-seen Capilano Lake, usually hidden from the public behind the fences of the watershed, now stands revealed with all of Vancouver below; beyond is the mountain of mountains, lofty Baker. Play the game of spotting familiar landmarks in your neighbourhood, especially near the magic evening hour when the air clears. It's tempting to think of spending a night up here. There is the occasional level site covered with thick grass on which you could stretch out. Nights get chilly, though, so you had better make sure you have your sweetie with you in your down bag. Being isolated from all the action makes the Lions one place where you don't want to be lonely.

5 | GAMBIER ISLAND

Gambier Island is just the right distance from Vancouver for an exotic ocean getaway with a decidedly rustic touch. If you go by B.C. Ferry, you must have the timing right in order to make all your connections, but if you choose to go by water taxi, you call the shots as to your departure time. Half the fun of going to Gambier is the boat ride on Howe Sound. The other half is the large island itself, which abounds with possibilities for easy outdoors enjoyment—especially walks through thick forests—free of crowds and intrusions.

Gambier is a rugged island with little room for agriculture. Much of its early history was taken up with logging. You see remnants in the massive cedar stumps that dot the forest floor, the number of decaying nurse logs from which have sprouted new generations of trees, and the maze of ancient logging roads now softened by green ground cover. Mature second growth prevails, lending a serene feeling to much of the island. Most homes are on the southwest corner of Gambier at New Brighton and Gambier Harbour. Regular ferry service connects the island to Langdale on the Sunshine Coast. Three popular church-run summer camps, Artaban, Fircom and Lantona, enjoy sun-washed sites on the deeply indented southeastern side. Otherwise, the inhospitably steep topography saves Gambier from being built up as a bedroom community for Vancouver, nearby Bowen Island's fate.

Your first clue to how Gambier differs from most of the southern Gulf Islands is discovering there's only foot-passenger ferry service. A small but powerful aluminum-hulled 38-seater, the *Dogwood Princess II*, spirits you across Thornbrough Channel to New Brighton and Gambier Harbour. On a blustery day you'll be in for a bumpy ride—sometimes I wonder about the fate of the first *Dogwood Princess*. (If you're travelling on a weekend, make sure to leave plenty of time to get in line at the wharf on Gambier for your return journey to Langdale. Occasionally, more people wish to leave the island at once than can be carried by the little ferry. An alternative for service out off-island would be to make arrangements with Gambier Island Water Taxi, 886-8321.)

Visiting the rural island in Howe Sound from Vancouver requires a 45-minute ferry ride to Langdale from Horseshoe Bay. (Allow extra time in Horseshoe Bay to find parking space for your vehicle. You can use the pay parking close to the ferry terminal for under $10 per day, or park for free farther uphill next to the highway overpass, a 10-minute walk.) From Langdale you have a 10-minute sprint on a second ferry from Langdale to the federal dock at New Brighton. Be quick about making the connection between the two ferries at Langdale, as the *Dogwood Princess* doesn't tarry for stragglers. Simply walk off the ferry at Langdale and you will find the well-marked ferry to Gambier docked immediately alongside.

On arrival at New Brighton you'll find that the dock is a very quiet place once the ferry has departed. You are now where you've worked and organized so hard to be. If you've forgotten anything, head to the nearby general store (the only corner store on the island), uphill and around to the right, following the road to Gambier Harbour. There are several crafts people with studios on Gambier; you might like to combine exploring the island with a visit to one or two of them as you make the rounds. You can find details on their whereabouts by visiting the store. Unfortunately, Gambier Island, lacking a chamber of commerce, does not publish a local map, but you'll find that signage, although not plentiful, is adequate at most crossings.

Walking up from the dock you'll see that the shoreline around the small cove is easily accessible. You may be tempted to pause here for a moment to get organized. You won't be hurting any property owner's feeling if you do, as all shoreline in the province is Crown land.

The main road divides almost immediately. Your choice for a day's outing on this corner of Gambier will take you either along the west side as far as Andys Bay in an hour, and farther along to Gambier Lake, a three-hour walk from New Brighton, or alternatively south to the road's end at Gambier Harbour. The latter offers the best choice of picnic spots, on the logs beside Whispering Creek.

ANDYS BAY AND GAMBIER LAKE   The road to Andys Bay is a shady one, half logging road, half country lane in places, and it can be muddy. Starting from New Brighton, follow the main road left past homes built up behind the beach. Bear right at the first fork in the road beyond the beach, walking back into the woods away from the ocean. The road narrows to a laneway for the next hour's journey, and the atmosphere is extremely conducive to leisurely walking and nature observation. Watch for the old road to divide again. Bear left here, following the marked trail to the next divide, which appears in 15 minutes. From here you can either descend to Andys Bay on the left, or carry on to a series of lakes tucked into the slopes of Mount Liddell. This section of the trail is well marked. It will take you another two hours to reach Gambier Lake from here. The return ferry schedule will help determine how much time you can spend exploring the west side of Gambier. (There are rough campsites at Gambier Lake if you wish to make an overnight journey.)

GAMBIER HARBOUR   A less demanding, more leisurely alternative to exploring Gambier's west side is to spend an afternoon strolling closer to the ferry dock. Whispering Creek flows into nearby Gambier Harbour, a 30-minute walk from New Brighton. In late October you can watch in fascination while hundreds of coho salmon struggle against the current as they make their way upstream to spawn. The views from the beach are of West Bay, one of four major indentations on the island's south side.

HALKETT BAY   Halkett Bay Marine Park is located on Gambier Island's sheltered southeast corner. With the acquisition of this 763-acre (309-ha) piece of island property by the provincial government in 1988, an entirely different side of Gambier opened for public exploration and enjoyment. You'll need a boat to reach Halkett Bay. Though the waters of Howe Sound may look decidedly calm on occasion, don't risk having the winds come up while paddling a small, open boat over to the island. Unless you

Island in Halkett Bay at low tide

approach Halkett by kayak from the private marina at Sunset Beach, 3 mi. (5 km) north of Horseshoe Bay, put your canoe or other car-top boat on a water taxi for the 20-minute ride out of Horseshoe Bay.

Mercury Launch and Tug (921-7451) is the only water taxi operating from Horseshoe Bay, with two large aluminum-hulled boats that leave from the government wharf. A one-way trip to Gambier is expensive—nearly $50—so to justify the expense gather as many friends or family members together for the journey as you can. (On the adjacent wharf, Sewell's Marina rents outboards by the hour. Phone 921-3474 for current rates.)

As you cross the choppy waters at the mouth of Howe Sound you quickly become entranced by the scenery. Rising above to the east is the Howe Sound Crest, with the extended ridge that runs from Black Mountain in West Vancouver north to the Lions. Busy Bowen Island is off the starboard side. You may wonder whether all the water traffic around Bowen will impinge on the serenity of your destination. Fortunately, the only marine sound that carries across the water comes from the occasional passage of the Sunshine Coast ferry. Once you're in Halkett Bay much of the Howe Sound Crest is hidden from view, obscured by the cliffs that rise on the east side of the bay.

With the creation of the marine park at Halkett Bay came the installation of a new government wharf at the landing. The bay once choked with logs is now more likely to feature a dozen or more boats anchored offshore. Most of the floating visitors are usually content to rest at anchor; once ashore you may well find that you have the campground and its surroundings to yourself.

A thick fringe of hemlock and second-growth fir shield the shoreline from view. As the water taxi pulls away—with instructions as to when you wish to be collected—you may wonder what lies in the forest at the end of the wharf. If you walk into the shade of the trees you'll discover a series of clearings linked by old logging trails that have assumed the character of sedate laneways. The only sign of earlier habitation is a long, swinging rope hanging from high above in the trees. This will provide constant amusement whenever you feel like taking a ride.

One pleasant surprise is the discovery of a fresh-water stream running nearby (nonetheless, your provisions should include a large container of fresh water). Another surprise will come when you go to explore the small island just offshore in the bay. It boasts a small beach, above which stands a clearing large enough for one tent. A bench has been built between the island's lone tree and an adjacent rock knoll. Beside it lies a stone fire-ring. Occasionally you'll find that the previous occupant has left a pile of neatly stacked driftwood, testimony that this is one place to safely enjoy a marshmallow roast. Otherwise, Halkett Bay has a posted ban on campfires.

When the tide is out a sandbar links Gambier's shore to the little island and you can walk there. On summer evenings this is a prime location from which to do some stargazing. You can often see flashes of summer lightning from the Fraser Valley glowing in the night sky like aurora borealis, though you'll rarely hear any thunder.

MOUNT ARTABAN　　For the best views of eastern Howe Sound from Gambier Island, undertake the 3-mi. (5-km), two-hour climb (one way) of nearby Mount Artaban. The modest elevation gain of 1968 ft. (600 m) makes this fairly easy to accomplish in the course of a half-day.

Follow the old logging road that terminates beside the campsites at Halkett Bay west to Camp Fircom, a half-hour walk. At first the road leads through the forest, but it descends to the shoreline as it nears the camp, with a pleasing view south of Bowen Island's Hood Point.

Walk through Camp Fircom to the caretaker's home on a rise at the back of the property, picking up the trail to Mount Artaban from behind his house. As the trail is frequently used by campers during summer months it is well kept and marked. Follow this trail—really a road in its early stages—and pass the turnoff on the left to Gambier Estates. Watch for the trail to Mount Artaban, marked by orange surveyor's tape, which branches off on the left where it skirts beside another housing development. The forest is open here, with many prize-size trees lining the way. Just making it this far is a reward in itself.

The trail begins to climb towards a long ridge, at the eastern end of which is Mount Artaban. The ascent, through a rock canyon, is one of the prettiest parts of the journey.

Once on top you'll find the remains of a fire-spotter's old cabin. Sitting on its run-down timbers you can see why it's located here: the views in all directions are uninterrupted. Howe Sound lies at your feet. Your eyes can sweep from Horseshoe Bay north to Britannia Beach, taking in Anvil Island and a series of tiny islets whose rocky heads protrude above the waters of the sound. On a clear day the view of the Howe Sound Crest is like a geography lesson. Directly east across the sound is Lions Bay. The west peak of the Lions is easily the most recognizable feature.

Just below the peak of Mount Artaban are two small ponds ringed by hemlock and cedar trees, a sheltered, shady place to picnic if you find the top too exposed to either sun or wind.

THE NORTH SHORE |

FUN BEGINS WHERE THE SIDEWALKS END

There's a lot happening on the North Shore that escapes notice from Vancouver. Cross over the Lions Gate or Second Narrows bridges to West or North Vancouver and you'll find a side of life long since past in the big city. Milk's not delivered in horse-drawn wagons any longer, but bear and cougar still put in an occasional appearance in North Shore backyards at higher elevations. Wildlife competes for turf with mountain bikers, who sneak up the slopes to cut secret trails for fun, and with bigger fish, such as the Greater Vancouver Regional District—quietly cutting champion old growth for profit in the watersheds that lie out of bounds and beyond public scrutiny.

One of the best books on the trees of this forest is Randy Stoltmann's *Hiking Guide to the Big Trees of Southwestern B.C.* (Western Canada Wilderness Committee, 1991). Since Pauline Johnson walked these trails with Chief Capilano in the early days of this century, writers have roamed the North Shore with delight, though rarely with such knowledgeable company as Johnson enjoyed. In the early 1980s Roger and Ethel Freeman meticulously documented and mapped this area in their book *Exploring Vancouver's North Shore Mountains* (Federation of Mountain Clubs of British Columbia, 1985)—unfortunately now out of print, but watch for it in secondhand-book stores.

When you look at the North Shore from down at sea level your eyes are drawn up to the peaks, checking for signs of fresh

Skiing Humpty Dumpty on Cypress

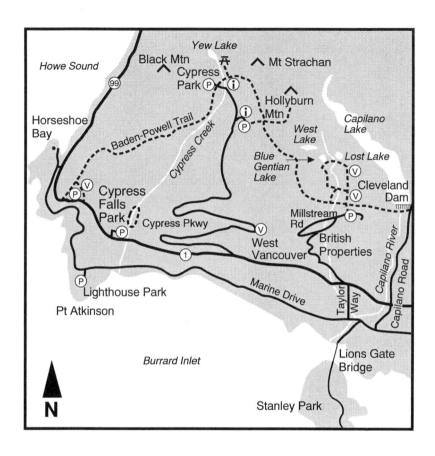

snow in winter and enviously eyeing the cool green forests in summer. The four destinations in this section invite you up there to explore the North Shore's pothole lakes and splashing streams, its towering trees and winding forest paths.

One trail that stands head and shoulders above the rest also knits West and North Vancouver together: the Baden-Powell trail, one of the Lower Mainland's most under-publicized recreational resources. Once you've been introduced to it, as well as the North Shore's two provincial parks—Cypress and Seymour—you'll have plenty of inspiration to return here at a moment's notice, such as the next time that the sun does or

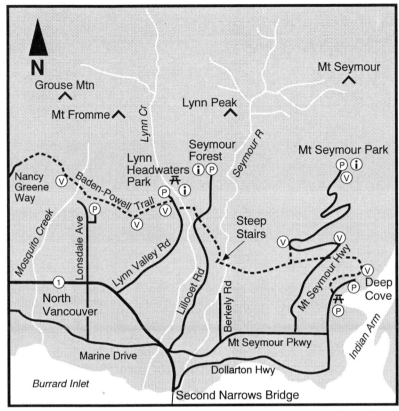

North Shore

doesn't shine. An old Vancouver saying has it that if you can't see the North Shore, it's raining, and if you can, then it's about to rain. A visit to the North Shore will keep a smile on your face no matter what's happening—with all this forest, it's a great rainy-day getaway.

6 | CYPRESS PROVINCIAL PARK

CYCLING ◄
DRIVING ◄
HIKING ◄
PICNICKING ◄
SKIING ◄
VIEWPOINTS ◄
WALKING ◄

With over a million visitors a year, Cypress Provincial Park in West Vancouver is the most popular destination of its kind in B.C. Stop on the drive up into the park or on the way down to admire the views of the Lower Mainland and Washington State from the Cypress Park viewpoint. These views, the park's proximity to the city and its easily accessible trails account for Cypress's prominence with the public.

Cypress Provincial Park was born out of controversy, and the tussles over its future continue as heatedly today as they have over the past three decades. Former B.C. premier Dave Barrett is the acknowledged saviour of Cypress. In 1975, during the last months of his NDP administration's term of office, Barrett stepped in to create a Class A park on land that had been logged in the 1960s, ostensibly for alpine ski runs. As anyone who lived in Vancouver at the time will recall, there was much skulduggery involved. Having made a mockery of the original plan by clear-cutting much of Black Mountain and Mount Strachan's upper slopes, Valley Royal, the company that had originally proposed the scheme, was unmasked under a cloud of allegations tying its finances to those of a Bahamian gambling syndicate.

B.C. Parks, attempting to make the best of a nightmarish situation, began operating Cypress Bowl as a public ski facility in the late 1970s. This did not last long. Cypress was caught up in the Social Credit government's plans to privatize a variety of government services within the Ministry of Lands, Parks and Public Housing (as it was then known), and the contract for both alpine and nordic skiing within the park was sold to Cypress Bowl Recreations Limited (CBRL) in 1984. Although private operators are not generally allowed in Class A parks, Cypress has a Category 6 designation, which permits recreational as well as conservational activities. Examples of where this has worked to everyone's satisfaction include Silver Star Provincial Park near Vernon, one of the Okanagan's best ski resorts, and, more recently, Blackcomb Glacier Provincial Park in Whistler.

You make your way into the 7400-acre (2996-ha) park, accessed from the Upper Levels Highway in West Vancouver, via a 5-mi. (8-km) paved highway. While most visitors ride up on four wheels, others make do with two, sometimes with a pair of skis strapped to the bicycle frame. On the way to the top (the road ends at Cypress Bowl) there are four major switchbacks. You'll usually see cars parked near each one. From the gate at the first switchback, the old Cypress Creek logging road leads west towards Cypress Falls Park, climbing from there to the parking lot at Cypress Bowl, a distance of 4.7 mi (7.6 km). The Cypress Park Viewpoint is at the second of the switchbacks. There is ample parking here and an accompanying interpretive sign that identifies the geographical landmarks laid out before your eyes. Just above the third switchback are two rough entrances to trails on the lower slopes of Hollyburn Mountain. The well-marked turnoff to the Hollyburn cross-country centre and its parking lot is located farther uphill. Cypress Bowl is just a short drive past the Hollyburn turnoff. In springtime, the snowbanks lining this last stretch of road become "Cypress Beach." Sun worshippers unfold their lawn chairs and picnic tables atop the towering mounds of snow pushed up by plows during the winter months, and soak up rays as part of an annual ritual welcoming the return of warm weather to the coast.

Long before chairlifts and alpine skiers came to Cypress Bowl, cross-country skiers enjoyed the trails on adjacent Hollyburn Mountain. In the 1920s and 1930s as many skiers trekked out around West Lake as do today. Hollyburn is the only one of the three mountains within Cypress Park that has not been logged. (Under a development proposal favoured by CBRL, the current alpine ski boundary would be extended and a portion of old-growth forest on the mountain's west side would be logged to create more trails.) One of Hollyburn's unique features is that it has the last accessible stand of giant hemlock in the Lower

Hollyburn Mountain viewpoint

Mainland between Garibaldi Provincial Park and Chilliwack. Add to this the fact that it hasn't been touched by forest fires in the past one to four millennia, and you have an environment that many persons passionately wish to preserve. Writer Randy Stoltmann has counted rings on a stump atop Mount Strachan that indicated it was nearly 1200 years old when cut in 1988 as part of a previous expansion.

HOLLYBURN SUMMIT   Hollyburn Mountain is best known for its popular cross-country ski trails; however, nordic activities here take up at most only half the calendar. The rest of the year, hiking boots make their mark on the trails that crisscross the slopes below the mountain's 4350-ft. (1326-m) peak. Hollyburn's companions, Mount Strachan to the north and Black Mountain to the west, stand at 4770 ft. (1454 m) and 4016 ft. (1224 m) respectively. Hollyburn's unlogged summit allows unimpeded views of the mountain ranges to the north, for the most part not visible from Vancouver. You can hike to the summit in less than two hours.

From the cross-country parking lot, head uphill underneath the hydro lines. A service road doubles as a trail for the stretch from the parking lot to the warming hut beside Third Lake (the hut is for winter use only, as are several of the privies that stand head and shoulders above the landscape without the benefit of snow to provide easy access). A kiosk at the trailhead on the east side of the parking lot features a detailed diagram of trails on Hollyburn. It also lays out a sensible approach to exploring all wilderness settings: dress warmly, always let someone know where you're going and when you can reasonably be expected back, and never hike the mountains alone.

After hiking for 15 minutes, most of it uphill, you'll reach the skiers' warming hut. Once at the crest of the hydro trail the approach to the warming hut begins to level off. At almost any time of the year, you'll find water running in the rocky creekbeds that double as trails on the mountain. Waterproof footwear is advisable but not absolutely necessary. You can see the open ski trails through the forest, with their names— Burfield, Sitzmark, Telemark, Wells Gray—posted high in the trees.

A trail marker beside the warming hut, announcing the approach to Hollyburn Mountain, bears a map of the area and a summary of distances and times. The warming hut is at 3586 ft. (1093 m), which means you have a 764-ft. (233-m) ascent ahead before you reach the summit. Once you set out, you'll find that the trail divides after about 15 minutes, with the Hollyburn trail heading straight ahead and the Baden-Powell trail branching off to the left toward the parking lot at Cypress Bowl, a 40-minute journey. The hike to the top of Hollyburn from this divide takes another 50 minutes.

As the trail climbs from the warming hut, it passes a series of six small lakes, four of which can be glimpsed from the trail. The trail leads along the shoreline of Fourth Lake several minutes past the warming hut, then begins to snake through the woods, traversing the forested slopes and coming out into the open on an old ski-trail cut. On the east side of the trail, weathered signs warn against trespassing into the restricted Capilano watershed, whose boundary is nearby.

As you climb, you won't be distracted by many views. Just watch your footing. As on many of the trails on Hollyburn—this one is maintained under the Adopt-a-Trail program by the Happy Trails Club—much of the way is over exposed roots around the base of the sturdy firs. (On the way down, you'll be treated to views galore out over the Fraser estuary as far south as Boundary Bay.)

Along the trail, you'll frequently catch sight of Hollyburn's beckoning summit, surmounted by a dense crown of old growth. Late in the summer berry bushes line the way; snow flattens them in winter, creating a challenging descent for those who've made the trek to this elevation. Just before the final ascent, where the going does get tricky in several places owing to rocks made slippery by running water or ice, a charming viewpoint appears, with a rustic bench. It's well situated for catching your breath *and* the geographical display. The sides of Hollyburn drop away into the Capilano Valley, hidden below. Rising vertically to the north and east are the walls of Grouse Mountain and its companions; in the distance are the peaks and ridges of Coliseum and Seymour mountains. Although the view from the top is more panoramic, it somehow can't match this setting. It must be the bench.

The actual peak of Hollyburn is open and rocky, an encouragement in the last 10 minutes of the hike when you can see the sky beginning to appear above you, no longer masked by trees. A dangling rope offers assistance to ascend the last steep rock section before the top, which is really only a matter of several footsteps beyond. If you've really pushed to get here, maybe with an incoming squall dogging your heels, you can at last catch your breath before hurrying back down. It feels as good to have accomplished this climb as it would if you'd mastered any other significant peak—remember, everyone has his or her own Everest within. From the summit you can look west to the top of the Collins chairlift on Mount Strachan, past Black Mountain to the waters of Howe Sound and over to Gibsons on the Sunshine Coast in the distance.

A rough, steep trail leads from the summit of Hollyburn to Mount Strachan. Rather than attempt this traverse, I recommend that you retrace your steps to the warming hut; if you've still got steam in your legs at this point, walk down the Wells Gray trail to First Lake, or follow the Mobraaten trail to its intersection with the Grand National trail, and around on Grand National to West Lake. Both Wells Gray and Mobraaten start from the warming hut and both intersect with Grand National. Part of an old chairlift can still be seen at the north end of West Lake.

For a flavour of the original development on Hollyburn begun in the 1920s, be sure to return to the parking lot on the Burfield trail, which passes beside a nest of old cabins.

OTHER DESTINATIONS   Cypress Bowl presents an opportunity for visitors to make easy, moderate or extensive explorations of the park. A short 0.9-mi. (1.5-km) interpretive trail leads from the parking lot to nearby Yew Lake. (Cypress Creek originates in the marshy wetland surrounding this lake.) This trail has been upgraded to provide wheelchair access and is also designed with visually impaired visitors in mind. Several picnic tables are situated in strategic locations with views west through the folds of Black Mountain to Howe Sound, and east to Mount Strachan and Hollyburn Mountain. Yellow cypress trees, from which the park takes its name, ring the little lake.

For those with more time and energy to burn, trails ascend Black Mountain to its summit, a 30-minute climb, or head north along the Howe Sound Crest trail towards the Lions and Deeks Lake, a one- or two-day trek. Even if you don't intend to go all the way to the Lions on this trail, several hours' hiking will bring you past good viewpoints leading up to St. Marks Peak, 3.4 mi. (5.5 km) from Cypress Bowl. Snow may cover parts of this trail, especially at higher elevations, well into July. North of St. Marks the trail deteriorates as it approaches aptly named Unnecessary Mountain. This may well be as far as you wish to come. More detailed information on the Howe Sound Crest trail is available on a special map designed for trail users by Jim Cuthbert, a Visitor Services officer with B.C. Parks. Call 924-2200 to receive a free copy of the map.

7 | CYPRESS FALLS PARK

Even in the depths of winter there are still times when a day trip is in order—if only to get you out of the house and away from the threat of cabin fever. Of all the ingredients that make for a good winter outing, proximity is paramount. Since the sun supplies us with only eight hours of daylight in December and January, choose a place that's close at hand so getting there doesn't waste precious time. Wind chill is another factor in the equation: the place you visit should be sheltered. Thirdly, your destination should catch nature displaying herself at her seasonal best.

One of the wintry manifestations I like most is the sight of frozen spray, layer upon layer of ice coating trees, rocks and earth like ceramic glaze. Cypress Creek in West Vancouver spills down the slopes of Black Mountain, creating just such an effect in two places where the water really falls. A small park surrounds one of the most dramatic sections of the creek. Viewpoints of the upper and lower falls are easily reached from the parking lot even when snow is deep and crisp.

Anyone who has travelled west along the Upper Levels Highway will have crossed Cypress Creek near the falls. A road sign marks the location of the creek, but the falls are hidden in a gorge, surrounded by the forest. Unless you know where to search them out, they remain a local secret. To find the park, take the Caulfeild-Woodgreen exit. Once on Woodgreen, follow around to the third street on the right, Woodgreen Place. There is no indication that the park lies at the end of this street, only a sign reading No Exit. A painted sign affixed high on a tree at

Cypress Falls in winter

the street's end points to a parking lot in an old quarry. Next to this are some tennis courts and a playing field. The trail to the falls begins here.

Ancient trails crisscross the banks around Cypress Falls. Although they're not as well marked as the Brothers Creek or Capilano-Pacific trails, finding your way is not difficult. There has been a minimum of logging on this part of the mountain, and trails stand out against the dense forest background as if nature herself were inviting visitors. In places there are stands of original growth that sprouted around Milton's time.

At some point in the past 400 years a fire swept across the face of Black Mountain (hence its name). You can still discern dark scars on the trunks of the older Douglas firs and Western hemlocks. Some of these trees tower nearly 230 ft. (70 m) above the forest floor. Their almost 10-ft. (3-m) girth means that you *really* have to stretch your arms to give them a full hug.

Walk down a staircase to the playing field, bearing to your left for a short distance towards some bleachers. From here the trail enters the woods in two directions. To reach the falls, head uphill on the left-hand trail. (The right-hand trail, suitable for jogging, is a soft bark-chip ring-trail that circles the field.) The sound of the creek will almost immediately impress itself on your ears.

The gentle rise of the trail makes it suitable for walkers of all ages, even in slippery wintery conditions. Stick to the trail that leads upwards rather than follow the small level roadbed closer to the creek. Parts of the trail can be mucky, so bring high-top footwear for this walk. Leave your cotton socks behind in winter, because when wet they will leach warmth out of your body 200 times faster than it can be replaced. Instead, wear wool, silk or polypropylene.

You'll come to a viewpoint of the lower falls within five minutes. The spray here coats the walls of the gorge as this part of the cataract drops away to a pool 56 ft. (17 m) below. There is a small fence here to prevent anyone from venturing too close. Otherwise, this is a very non-threatening version of the Capilano Canyon. No need to worry about slipping. A bridge crosses over to the east side of the creek. Just beyond, roots from a stand of old-growth forest hold the mountainside together. This is the steepest part of the park. Instead of crossing Cypress Creek at this point, I recommend staying on the west bank, travelling in a clockwise direction to the upper falls and crossing here on your return.

Keep close to the creek as the trail rises gradually on the west bank. Smaller trails occasionally cut off up to the left, allowing neighbourhood access to the creek. The main trail is demarcated by wooden railings in places. No matter where you might turn, as long as you can hear the creek clearly you can't go wrong.

You may have to backtrack, but you should have no trouble finding the right path. In an easy 40 minutes you will have reached the upper falls viewpoint.

There are two magnificent old Douglas fir trees rising next to this viewpoint. On the forest floor below them a network of roots stands out, gleaming black as if lacquered. Up above, the broad spreading limbs catch much of the snow (or rain), keeping it from reaching the trail. Where snow does appear on the ground, it stands out in contrast to the reddish-brown bark and leaf mulch. When the outer boughs are coated with white, the interior limbs of many trees are sparkling green. Ferns persist where all else has perished from the frost. The odd holly tree with its spiky leaves puts the finishing touch on this seasonal scene.

The trail climbs again for a short distance beyond the upper falls viewpoint. A stand of young hemlocks line the trail on either side. You may have to move sideways between them in order to keep snow from dislodging and finding its way down your collar. All of a sudden your surroundings are brighter, a break from the twilight of the deep forest. If you want pictures you will have to use a high-speed film, a tripod or a flash to capture an impression.

Turn right onto the wide roadbed of an old logging road that climbs to the McCrady Bridge; from the bridge you can look down into the gorge carved by Cypress Creek's relentless flow. The road runs downhill past a hydro substation. Pick up the trail back to the lower falls on your right, just after you pass the humming wires. It is marked by three metal flags, the only signage on this walk. (If you stay on the logging road it will take you east to the Cypress Parkway, 0.7 mi./1.1 km away.) Pick your way carefully down through this section and you will be at the lower falls bridge in 15 minutes. The round trip takes an easy two hours, by which time you should be ready for a hot toddy to warm your heart's cockles.

You can travel to Cypress Falls Park on West Van Transit. Take the Cypress Park bus (#253), which leaves from Park Royal at 20 minutes past each hour. For more information, call 985-7777.

8 | BROTHERS CREEK

CYCLING ◄
HIKING ◄
PICNICKING ◄
SWIMMING ◄
WALKING ◄

Sometimes it seems that we have discovered everything there is to know about our North Shore mountains. There can't be much of this territory that hasn't been walked through at least once. At the turn of the century there was no such certainty: when the little settlement of Ambleside was hardly more than a few cabins in size, residents had to guess at the origins of several creeks that flowed into the Capilano River from on high. The First Nations people who lived nearby could offer little more information, as they observed an ancient taboo against climbing in the mountains.

So it was that by the 1920s at least four creeks in the region came to be known as Sisters Creek. Speculation had it that each could trace its headwaters to the run-off from the Sisters, the twin peaks that today are referred to by the non-native community as the Lions. Finally, a provincial park survey team went to work. They determined that Sisters Creek ought to be the small, rather insignificant stream that flows into the north end of Capilano Lake (now off limits to the public as it is in the restricted Greater Vancouver Water Supply Area). The remaining streams were rechristened. One of the larger ones became Brothers Creek.

An exciting network of trails follow Brothers Creek on the mountainside above the British Properties. As a reward for overheated hikers there are two small lakes near the creek's origins. Getting to the trailhead can be accomplished in 20 minutes from downtown by driving to the top of Millstream in West Vancouver via Eyremont Drive where it intersects with Henlow Road.

Brothers Creek trail

As you would expect in the well-ordered municipality of West Vancouver, the trail is marked by a large wooden signpost. There is room in front of the yellow gate for several cars to park. Nearby is a bus stop. If you travel as a foot passenger, catch the #254 British Properties bus, which leaves Park Royal at 20 minutes before the hour. Check with West Van Transit (985-7777) for more details.

Depending on your time and hiking companions, a visit to Brothers Creek can last anywhere from an hour to a half-day. With the network of trails around the creek it's possible to tailor a visit here to fit any circumstance and any age group.

A rocky old fire road serves as the beginning of the Brothers Creek trail, no matter which variation you attempt. Take a good look at the scenery below as you set out on this trail—in a matter of minutes the tall trees will close in around you, shutting out all signs of the city until your return. Soon only an occasional sound—perhaps the whistle from the Royal Hudson steam locomotive in the B.C. Rail yards—will float up from the world you've left behind. Almost immediately the past will rise to greet you. Thick wooden planks used in the construction of skid roads are still evident in places. They are studded with heavy spikes and act as reminders, along with some enormous cedar stumps sprinkled throughout the forest, of the logging activity here 70 years ago.

Within minutes of starting the trail you are presented with a choice of routes. Three bridges cross Brothers Creek, approximately 20 minutes' walk apart. You might follow soft and mostly level Baden-Powell trail west to the first of these if your time is limited. The trail parallels a power line and features a number of small boardwalks. Watch for a tall snag that stands out above the forest just as the trail begins its descent to quaint First Bridge. The round trip to this point is one hour.

From First Bridge the Brothers Creek trail climbs beside the creek with staircases built into the slope to assist you. A number of sheltering western red cedars stand on the west side of the creek. They'll amaze you with their girth. Who would have thought big trees such as these could exist so close to the city? (As it happens, some of the largest trees on the west coast grow in the nearby Capilano and Seymour watersheds, restricted areas since the 1920s. However, logging continues in the watershed, threatening these trees and raising concerns for the well-being of our water supply.) If you circle back over Second Bridge, rejoining the fire road, you will have had a brief but stimulating two-hour introduction to the area. Along the way between Second Bridge and the fire road is a stand of old-growth fir trees. These escaped the saw blade because they were too tall for early loggers to handle. Though not as dramatic as the fir and cedar higher up the slope near Third Bridge, they are still mighty impressive. There are also a number of blowdowns in this area, victims of a powerful local windstorm that struck in early May 1990.

If you have another hour or two at your disposal there's a most rewarding adventure in store. After climbing up the fire road or the trail beside Brothers Creek to Third Bridge, follow the trail markers to Blue Gentian Lake. This small lake lies on the west side of the creek, a half-hour above Third Bridge. There are two picnic tables beside its shore. Lily pads dot its surface and, in truth, it more closely resembles a pond than a lake. Small Stoney Creek can be heard nearby.

To complete a circle trip, follow an older trail that cuts east across both Stoney and Brothers creeks to Lost Lake. Somewhat larger and more inviting, it takes 20 minutes of up-and-downing to reach. If it's a warm day, have a swim in the fresh water under the open sky. A shorter approach to Lost Lake runs from Third Bridge: simply follow the trail on the east side of Brothers Creek. This takes only 15 minutes, but then you will have to retrace your footsteps. One of the rewards of using the circle route to both lakes is the view of the upper falls on Brothers Creek that appears only between the two.

Across the fire road below Third Bridge are the tallest stands of trees on the entire journey. Some of the firs and cedars measure 8 ft. (2.4 m) in diameter. Many of the tops have been snapped off, but green life persists in the remaining branches.

Each time I visit Brothers Creek I end up exploring farther. It's a perfect spot to escape the heat of the day or the falling rain, so well does its canopy of trees shelter visitors. The forest swallows you up, and it's not until you return to the trailhead that the city will intrude on your consciousness once more.

9 | BADEN-POWELL TRAIL

CAMPING ◄
CYCLING ◄
HIKING ◄
PICNICKING ◄
VIEWPOINTS ◄
WALKING ◄

Back in the heady days of 1967, when Canada was 100 years young, an enthusiasm for centennial projects swept through communities from coast to coast to coast. Three decades later, wherever you travel in this country you still encounter signs of this celebratory zeal: centennial arenas, parks, trails and a host of other civic endeavours. British Columbia's provincial centennial occurred in 1971, only four years later, and the infectious building spirit carried over locally. Thus, in certain instances, which centennial was actually being commemorated can be somewhat confusing. Take the case of the Baden-Powell Centennial trail on Vancouver's North Shore. The seeds for this development were sown in 1967, but construction of the trail officially began in 1971. In this case, you can sense an acknowledgement of both occasions in one project.

Anyone with a background in the scouting movement will be familiar with the name Baden-Powell. Honoured with a peerage for his adroit leadership of British troops during the siege of Mafeking in the Second Boer War, Robert Stephenson Smyth, 1st Baron Baden-Powell, went on to found the Boy Scouts in 1908, taking his inspiration from Canadian writer and naturalist Ernest Thompson Seton. He and his sister Agnes also founded the Girl Guides in 1910. To honour their memories and to mark B.C.'s centennial year, local Scout and Guide troops undertook the construction of a trail across the North Shore mountains from Deep Cove to Horseshoe Bay, a distance of almost 30 mi. (48 km).

Although it is possible to cover the entire Baden-Powell trail

Winter lookout on the Baden-Powell trail

in less than a day (theoretically it can be done in 18 hours), this was not the original intention. Most of the trail, with the exception of the challenging Black Mountain section near its western terminus, can be divided into easily digested pieces of several hours each.

The Scouts and Guides originally planned to have the trail run close to seven major access points, such as the British

Properties in West Vancouver and the top of Lonsdale Avenue in North Vancouver, where local residents or visitors arriving by car or public transit could have easy access for an hour or two's enjoyment. There are now 12 such entries to the trail. For those who wish to make a weekend of it, there are a limited number of campsites along the route. These are in clearings where the views south and west out over the Lower Mainland are enchanting, despite the distant road hum of reverberating engines and rubber tires. However, you must receive permission from the municipality of North Vancouver to camp (987-2622).

White trailhead signs and maps with distances and estimated completion times are highly visible and posted at convenient intervals. Many of the maps also show companion trails that intersect with the Baden-Powell. As well, orange metal markers nailed to trees help guide the way. In most places, these markers are hardly necessary—by now, the Baden-Powell trail is well worn by hikers and cyclists. (The Scouts and Guides maintained the trail for more than a decade after its completion, but its upkeep has fallen recently to a variety of local groups under the auspices of the Adopt-a-Trail program.)

Following are some highlights of the Baden-Powell trail, to help you determine which parts of the route you might enjoy on a day's outing. My approach to the Baden-Powell trail is similar to the one I take when I trace the Nicomekl River from its source in Langley to its eventual rendezvous with the Pacific: I arrange to go as part of a group, leaving a vehicle at each end of a section. Another approach, designed for those of us who dislike retracing our footsteps, is to tie in a section of the Baden-Powell with another of the North Shore trails, such as the ones around Brothers Creek, Lynn Creek or Mount Seymour, and then loop back to where we began.

EAGLERIDGE DRIVE TO BRITISH PROPERTIES   The western terminus of the Baden-Powell trail is on the east side of the Squamish Highway at Horseshoe Bay, at the north end of Eagleridge Drive. There's a large cleared area, which usually contains at least one parked car, by the trailhead. With several delightful viewpoints and easy walking for the first hour, this 5.3-mi. (8.5-km) section of the trail runs up the face of Black Mountain to the aptly named Eagle Ridge and over into Cypress Provincial Park. This is by far the most daunting section of the entire Baden-Powell trail. A piece of graffiti on one of the signposts just before the steepest section sums up the challenge; beneath "Eagle Bluff 60 Min. Steep Trail Ahead" some wit has scratched "All Scouts turn back." As demanding as any other trail in the region, including the hike to the Lions, Eagle Ridge should be attempted only by those in good physical condition.

As the trail runs east of the Cypress Bowl ski area in Cypress Provincial Park, it smooths out. From here to the British Properties is 6 mi. (9.5 km), which can be covered in four hours, one way. This is a good section to explore when you can make arrangements to leave a vehicle at each end, trading keys at a prearranged rendezvous point.

HOLLYBURN MOUNTAIN TO BRITISH PROPERTIES Much of the trail east of Cypress Bowl is around Hollyburn Mountain. Pick up the trail on the hillside above Parking Lot No. 2, beside the ski patrol's first-aid station. It's a 40-minute ramble around the west side of Hollyburn to a junction with the Hollyburn Mountain trail. From here the Baden-Powell descends the Pacific Run ski trail, passing a series of small lakes on its way towards the hydro cut. At this point it assumes the identity of the Wells Gray trail. Follow this downhill to First Lake, then swing east on Grand National trail. You may have to look high up in the trees to spot the trail markers, a good indication of how deep the snow gets this high on the mountainside. After a short stretch of fairly level terrain leading over to the site of the old Cypress Resort, destroyed by fire in the 1980s, the Baden-Powell trail descends once more, following Lawson Creek first on its west side, then for a greater length on its east. At this point you've come almost 5 mi. (8 km) from Cypress Bowl. From here east it's an easy 1 mi. (1.6 km) across Brothers Creek and along the hydro line corridor to the top of the British Properties.

Although there is no regular bus service to Cypress Park, there is hourly service from Park Royal to the stop on Millstream Road in the British Properties. From here the Baden-Powell trail is a 10-minute walk uphill on the fire road that also connects with the network of trails surrounding Brothers Creek.

BRITISH PROPERTIES TO CLEVELAND DAM The Baden-Powell trail makes its way briefly through the British Properties, crossing five streets in the neighbourhood before regaining its wilderness aspect. A relatively easy section begins at the intersection of

Bonnymuir and Glenmore in the British Properties. Here the way is open, in contrast to the sheltered forest environment characteristic of the remainder of this short trail. It's just under 1 mi. (1.4 km), so you need budget only 20 minutes to do it one way. Good views of Capilano Lake at the foot of Grouse Mountain are the chief reward, plus a look into the canyon at the foot of the hill as the trail passes through Capilano Park. Watch for kayakers in the river below as you cross the Cleveland Dam. It's tempting to explore the trails that lead south beside Capilano Canyon. This could be a day's destination in itself.

CLEVELAND DAM TO LYNN VALLEY ROAD   From the Cleveland Dam the Baden-Powell trail joins Nancy Greene Way as it leads 1 mi. (1.6 km) up to the Grouse Mountain Skyride, an easy if not sensational half-hour walk. There is regular bus service to Grouse Mountain on the #232 Queens from the Phibbs Exchange in North Vancouver.

Moving east of the Grouse Mountain parking lot, the Baden-Powell trail begins an almost uninterrupted ramble to its terminus in Deep Cove. There is a continuity to the terrain along the way between Grouse Mountain and Lynn Creek: tall second growth, a myriad of little creeks, sections that are mud-filled during the rainy seasons and across which you walk with great care—many of the wooden structures along the way are beginning to show their age. In several places large bridges and staircases have recently been rebuilt with newer, safer materials.

The 1.5-mi. (2.5-km) section between Grouse Mountain's Skyride and the old Grouse Mountain chairlift takes an hour to cover one way. The old chairlift cut scars Grouse Mountain at the top of Skyline Drive. A gate bars vehicle access from Skyline to the fire road. There is a maze of trails here on the west side of Mosquito Creek, with two separate entrances to the Baden-Powell trail leading east of the fire road, both well marked. (Over the course of its history the original Baden-Powell trail route has been changed to better adapt to the rugged terrain on the North Shore. In the area around the old chairlift are both old and new sections of the trail, all clearly identified.)

Take it easy crossing Mosquito Creek, where the trail descends to one of the biggest bridges on the entire route. Mosquito Creek, like Lynn Creek and the Seymour River, carves its way through rock canyon walls in its steepest, narrowest sections. The sound of water running high through these canyons is dynamic.

East of Mosquito Creek the Baden-Powell trail begins a straightforward traverse of the shoulder of Grouse Mountain and the steep slopes of Mount Fromme, albeit with enough ups and downs for constant variety.

Wooden benches carved from old tree trunks are positioned along the way at strategic, if infrequent, viewpoints. Otherwise, your vision is restricted by the density of the forest to the path in front of you. You are now on one of the longer stretches of the trail, as you pass above the uppermost neighbourhoods in North Vancouver, covering 3.4 mi. (5.5 km) from the top of Skyline to the top of Mountain Highway. Plan on taking two hours to complete this section. (There is one very fine campsite on this section, located at the viewpoint near Kilmer Creek.)

East of Mountain Highway the Baden-Powell trail skirts a new housing development that recently forced the rerouting of the original trail. The trail crosses the top of Hoskins, then descends to join the Lynn Valley Road near the entrance to Lynn Headwaters Regional Park. You can take the #229 Westlynn bus from Lonsdale Quay to here on Upper Lynn Valley Road.

LYNN VALLEY ROAD TO HYANNIS ROAD   Walk south along Lynn Valley Road to Dempsey Road where the trail picks up again, leading south to the Lynn Canyon Suspension Bridge. The Lynn Canyon Ecology Centre enjoys a location second to none, nestled beneath a sheltered grove, set back from the edge of the rocky furrow carved by Lynn Creek. The trail descends along the rim of the canyon to a sturdy suspension bridge. Crossing it is thrilling. This part of the canyon is a notoriously dangerous area for swimming. Just looking into its depths is dizzying enough.

Having climbed down to the bridge, it's now time to climb back up the east side of Lynn Canyon—not as difficult as it sounds, but a steady climb nonetheless, with the sounds of Lynn Creek urging you on. By the time you reach Lillooet Road, about 30 minutes later, you will have come 2.8 mi. (4.5 km) from Lynn Valley Road.

This next section of the trail is marked by large signposts on each side of Lillooet Road, located 0.8 mi. (1.3 km) north of the first of two gates controlling access to the Seymour Demonstration Forest. Crossing from one side of Lillooet Road to the other is a study in contrasts. Whereas Lynn Canyon is a sheltered area with some magnificent older fir trees and maples that turn bright gold and bleached white in autumn, the trail to the east side of Lillooet Road passes through a forest of an altogether different appearance—modest compared to the scale of Lynn Canyon—as it leads up a set of hefty stairs. The trees clear for a short distance as the trail crosses a ridge below Lynn Peak and then descends a set of steep staircases to a pipeline bridge crossing the Seymour River. This area is less popular with visitors than nearby Lynn Creek but no less impressive. From Lillooet Road east across the Seymour to Hyannis Road is only 0.7 mi. (1.2 km) and easily accomplished in under an hour.

The Baden-Powell trail climbs from the Seymour River, briefly passing through the neighbourhood around Hyannis Road. It follows beside a small creek, which has cut a course through a little valley. (You can take the Berkley bus to here.) Although not on the trail itself, a short 0.3-mi. (0.5-km) detour along Hyannis to Hill Drive and then up to the top of Blairview Road will not only yield an outstanding view of Vancouver's inner harbour and across the Strait of Georgia to distant Vancouver Island, but will also tie you in to a well-marked secondary trail that leads back to the Baden-Powell trail, a 15-minute side trip. With so few viewpoints on the Baden-Powell itself, try to fit this one in while you're on this leg of the trail.

HYANNIS ROAD TO MOUNT SEYMOUR ROAD East of Hyannis the Baden-Powell trail runs towards Deep Cove, passing through Mount Seymour Provincial Park, a distance of 4.5 mi. (7.2 km). You can budget four hours to complete it as a whole, or easily break it into two separate bites. Although there are no major creeks or rivers to cross, plenty of small brooks and streams carry moisture down off the slopes of Mount Seymour. Many are bridged, but you can expect to do a little rock-hopping across others.

Starting east from Hyannis and the Seymour River, it takes an easy two hours to reach the parking area and picnic grounds at the Baden-Powell trail's junction with Mount Seymour Road. Before reaching it you should make a detour where the Baden-Powell and Mushroom trails meet (a metal trailmarker indicates that this is 26 mi./42 km east of Horseshoe Bay). If you've been walking east of Hyannis you reach this intersection in an hour. If you've left your car at the Baden-Powell entrance on Mount Seymour Road, the Mushroom trail is a 30-minute walk west.

Mount Seymour lookout

The historic Mushroom parking lot is 15 minutes uphill from the Baden-Powell trail. It's marked by a sign that explains the important role once played by this site, where travellers to cabins on Mount Seymour left their vehicles before proceeding on foot. Almost overgrown by moss, ferns and alder now, an aging picket fence surrounds the cedar stump to which a mushroom-shaped notice board was once affixed. A short distance beyond the Mushroom parking lot is the Vancouver Lookout picnic ground, a great place to take a break after making the effort to get this far.

To rejoin the Baden-Powell trail, simply retrace your steps, or take the Buck access trail—a joy of a trail, overflowing with green essences—east from the Vancouver Lookout parking lot to where it joins the Old Buck trail, a 25-minute journey. Old

Buck trail is outlined with stones as it descends a staircased logging road, then narrows to a single-person trail just before meeting Mount Seymour Road. Cross the road to rejoin Old Buck trail, restored here to its original width. Although gated against vehicular traffic, this is part of the bicycle trail system in Mount Seymour Provincial Park where many of the pathways are open for riding. Descend to the intersection with the Baden-Powell trail, 15 minutes from the Buck access trail junction. Mount Seymour Road is 10 minutes east of here. If you want to connect with a bus you can follow Old Buck trail 1.4 mi. (2.2 km) downhill to the park headquarters. Buses stop on nearby Mount Seymour Parkway.

MOUNT SEYMOUR ROAD TO DEEP COVE   East of the parking lot on Mount Seymour Road, the Baden-Powell trail enters a much rougher section than the smooth trail west to Hyannis. In the short distance between Mount Seymour and Indian River Road there are boardwalks, bridges, stairs and a ladder to negotiate. Go left at Indian River Road for a short way to where the trail picks up again beneath the hydro lines. From here east is one of the prettiest sections as the views of Indian Arm open up. There is one particularly rewarding location atop an open cliff, worth the scramble up beneath the hydro lines for its views of both Indian Arm and Burrard Inlet.

Having gone as far east as possible, the Baden-Powell trail cuts south towards Deep Cove. In an hour you'll be out at its terminus on Panorama Drive, a short distance north of Gallant Avenue. This is as good a place as any to begin or end a visit to the trail, with a park, a pub and coffee shops nearby. At busy times there's still ample parking in the lot just south of the beach. The #211 Seymour and #212 Dollarton buses stop at the end of Gallant.

Deep Cove has changed considerably in the years since the Baden-Powell trail was built. As well as being a jumping-off point for explorers heading up Indian Arm, it has a spruced-up main street and a reputable bicycle shop, handy if you're in need of advice or repairs.

You can get a free map of the Baden-Powell trail from Scout House at 664 West Broadway in Vancouver (telephone 879-5721).

THE FRASER VALLEY |

SEIZE THE DAY!

It has always seemed to me that one of the greatest benefits that Canada derived from an international boundary decision was the fixing of the 49th parallel by the Treaty of Washington in 1846. If the line had been drawn even one degree farther north we would have been deprived of the Fraser Valley and it would have been us—not the Americans—bumped up against the mountain ranges that shadow each side of the valley.

If you care to validate this perspective, cross the border at Huntington-Sumas near Abbotsford and drive into the Cascade Mountains heaved up around Mount Baker. Look back across the Fraser Valley: imagine this being Washington State and not British Columbia. Then you'll realize (if you hadn't already) the tremendous good fortune we enjoy by having the valley as *our* recreational, agricultural and industrial resource.

Of course, it's ours only in trusteeship. Nature can claim it back with a shrug if the clash of tectonic plates produces a large enough earthquake, or if changing weather patterns, such as the onset of another ice age, render this fertile valley as uninhabitable as it was 10,000 years ago.

According to evidence recently unearthed in the Mission-Hatzic region, native peoples began to settle the Fraser Valley about 8000 years ago. During summer months you can visit the excavation taking place around Hatzic Rock, just north of the Lougheed Highway, to see the preserved timbers of an ancient longhouse for yourself. Just ask for directions at the Tourist Info Centre on your way through Mission. The site itself is marked by an enormous erratic boulder that sits in a nearby field.

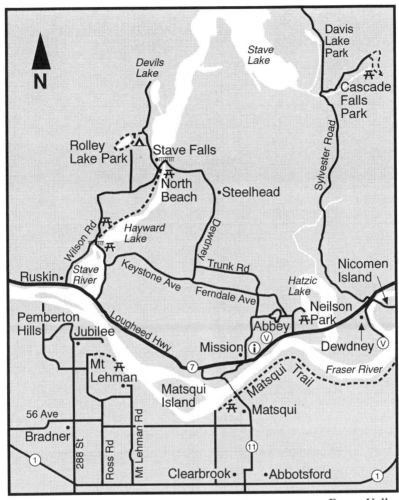

Fraser Valley

While the floor of the Fraser Valley is mostly taken up by farming, the surrounding hillsides are dotted with lakes and interlaced with hidden back roads where it seems residents have retreated to escape the rush of traffic on major routes such as the Trans-Canada and Loughheed highways. For day trippers from the city, these asphalt arteries are our quick-access tickets to valley hideaways such as Rolley and Cultus lakes, but there's one major drawback: when the highways become clogged with traffic all headed in the same direction, gridlock is inevitable. That's why I counsel readers to plan trips for off-peak times.

View of Mission from the abbey lookout

Leisure hours are some of the most precious at our disposal, and it's a shame to waste them staring at the bumper of the vehicle in front of you. Be flexible. Don't be afraid to get an early-morning jump on the rest of the world: remember, you can always nap once you're on site. *Carpe diem!*

10 | ROLLEY LAKE PROVINCIAL PARK

CAMPING ◄
FISHING ◄
HIKING ◄
ICE FISHING ◄
ICE SKATING ◄
NATURE OBSERVATION ◄
PADDLING ◄
PICNICKING ◄
SWIMMING ◄
WINTER CAMPING ◄

When the end of summer signals the return of campers to the city, the woods and lakes nearby welcome the return of the wildlife that spent the past few months in northern seclusion. Large birds such as eagles and Pacific loons are back with youngsters grown almost as big as their parents.

What's that sound? It's the voice of the wilderness, come back to take over your consciousness again for a while. Now is the time for a leisurely drive along some Fraser Valley back roads. Stop beside a secluded lake, or walk a riverside trail to see some fallen leaves being swept over a waterfall. Take a quiet moment to hear the Great Mystery speaking from the depths of a cedar forest.

You'll find just the place in the wooded hills of the Mission District east of Maple Ridge, at Rolley Lake Provincial Park. This little lake lies 43 mi. (70 km) east of Vancouver and is most easily reached by travelling on the Lougheed Highway (Highway 7). Traffic on the Lougheed can be stop and go until it reaches the Pitt River; you can avoid this by using the Trans-Canada (Highway 1) to link up with Lougheed at the Pitt River Bridge. Travelling east of Vancouver on the Trans-Canada, take exit 44 just before the highway crosses the Port Mann Bridge, and then head east on the Mary Hill Bypass road towards Maple Ridge and Mission.

Once on Highway 7 you can again save yourself a few minutes by taking the Haney Bypass through Maple Ridge. Watch for the large overhead sign indicating a right turn off Highway 7 towards Mission. The bypass rejoins Highway 7 east of Maple Ridge, and you are well on your way to Rolley Lake and the Stave Lake region. The highway follows the curves of the Fraser River. East of Maple Ridge the countryside becomes noticeably less populated. The well-marked turnoff to Rolley Lake is at the mill town of Ruskin and lies 6 mi. (10 km) north of Highway 7. Before reaching Ruskin the highway passes beside the small river towns of Albion and Whonnock.

After turning off Highway 7 you will be driving uphill past the Ruskin dam to an intersection with the Dewdney Trunk Road. At the sign here turn right and drive east to Bell Road, where a sign reads "Rolley Lake 2 km." Turn left here.

At this point you are just east overland of Alouette Lake and the Blue Mountain Forest. Rolley Lake has been a provincial park since 1961, and you may have noticed signs for it as you've driven east on Highway 7, but perhaps it seemed too close to the ever-widening development in the Haney region to have retained any of its wild side.

Any preconceived notions will evaporate like morning mist on the day when you finally do arrive. Here is a small lake with nothing hidden around its circumference except the 65 campsites (six of which are double-occupancy) in the nearby woods, several minutes' walk from the shoreline. Thus, Rolley Lake is as much a preserve of day trippers as it is of campers.

Part of the charm of driving up to the lake is passing the many old and new homes and farms along the paved back roads that climb through the hills above Ruskin. Many visitors will be charmed by the appearance of the well-kept houses and spacious gardens and perhaps be lured to settle here themselves. From our Vancouver perspective, "reclusive" is the word that comes to mind as you imagine living here. Yet the pressure to develop and urbanize this region may spark major changes before the turn of the century.

Settlers such as James and Fanny Rolley first began arriving in the 1880s. The couple to whom the lake owes its name homesteaded here for a decade before moving to nearby Whonnock. Remains of the logging camps that took over and cleared off most of the cedar are still evident around the lake's western perimeter. The Japanese crew that worked much of the forest pulled out in the 1930s when the last of the red cedars and Douglas firs were gone. An ancient corduroy road, along which logs were hauled to old Port Haney, is in remarkably good

Trail beside Rolley Lake falls

condition, considering the passage of time. You can see signs of the road when you walk the trail that begins west of the day parking lot and leads past the outhouses set back in the woods behind the beach. This trail soon turns into the old corduroy road. Remains of rotting cedar shakes let you know you're in the right place.

In the 60 years since, the forest around Rolley Lake has

regrown amid what's left of the old growth. Fallen nurse logs, each supporting three or four offspring, are slowly repopulating the forest floor. A boardwalk trail leads across a wet zone at the southwestern end of the lake, away from a modest-sized beach and picnic area. Here, in the stillness, a practised eye can identify dozens of species of birds in the course of a 90-minute walk around the lake. Pileated woodpeckers with their distinctive red heads (*pileated* is derived from the Latin *pileus*, meaning "felt cap") are among the winged residents often spotted.

A steep slope climbs above Rolley Lake's shady north side. Several small streams flow down off the hillside at wet times of the year. The water is a deep red, tinted by the cedar mulch through which it runs. At intervals along this side of the lake, small wooden docks float under a canopy of long hemlock boughs, making ideal places to fish for rainbow and cutthroat trout or to use those binoculars to search out the profiles of herons standing sentinel in the marsh at the lake's northeastern corner. The catch allowance (for humans) is two per day; there is no limit on the amount of fun that young and old alike can share while tossing in a line. You can park yourself on one of the docks to enjoy the stillness, with no fear of being interrupted by the sounds of outboards—no motorized boats are allowed on the lake.

The campsites at Rolley Lake seem exceptionally spacious compared to those at many other parks in B.C. Much of the surrounding forest is a mix of western hemlock and mature vine maple. The forest floor is open, and soft underfoot from centuries of cedar mulch. Children will find plenty of material for the construction of small forts and lean-tos in the underbrush. The vine maples naturally bend to form shelters that look surprisingly similar to the framework of Indian sweat lodges. Note that the use of sticks and underbrush from campground and park areas for fires and tent structures is not permitted.

During warm-weather months from early spring through midfall, a campsite costs about $15 per day, with a limit of 14 days on occupancy. This is an extremely popular park and space is at a premium during many weekends. But you will have the place practically to yourself at most other times, such as those special days in May and September before school ends or after it has reconvened. Each site comes furnished with a bright yellow cedar picnic table and fire-pit with cooking grill. The campsites are clean and there is plenty of water (though it's slightly sulphurous in smell) and firewood, with indoor toilets and tiled showers next to a children's adventure playground.

As you sit quietly, listen for the soft peeping of the bushtits, flocks of whom come by to feed on insects. You'll hear them before you spot their dark shapes high in the boughs of the hemlocks. They drop from branch to branch, hanging upside-down as easily as right side up, moving, in the words of Roger Tory Peterson, "from bush to tree in straggling flocks." Another visitor, one of the early risers, is the Douglas squirrel, as black as the back of the Steller's jay who'll be by later in the day to clean any leftover crumbs from your table. In the mountains north of Rolley Lake are far larger species of wildlife, such as black bears, so be careful to pack all food away at night. On a large-scale map of the province you can see that a wilderness corridor, in which large and small animals have dominion, stretches from here north past Harrison Lake and all the way to Lillooet.

While you're here there's a good chance of meeting Al Grass, one of the pillars of the B.C. Parks system, a veteran of years at Rolley Lake. During the summer months, he shares his extensive knowledge of the forest with visitors to the park's interpretive centre. Perhaps you'll find him with a book in hand, maybe one that gives a close-up look at the giant forest slug of western North America. Grass holds a real appreciation for this small mollusk, whose work as one of nature's ardent recyclers is clearly underrated, misunderstood and overdue for re-evaluation. At his workshops, Grass finds that young children are especially inspired when they see the slug as part of a grand scheme to keep the forests clean. If, in Al Grass's eyes, you prove to be quality material, you may even be invested as a member of "Jerry's Rangers," Al's conservation group, whose mascot is Jerry the Moose.

Before you leave Rolley Lake, follow the small stream that drains from its northeastern end down into nearby Stave Lake. A waterfall drops away through the forest in several stages, each more dramatic than the one before. To find it, take the path from the lake to the camping area. The walk begins at campsite 27 and takes an easy 10 minutes. After crossing the stream below the first set of falls you enter a recently clearcut area of the Stave forest. Wild black and red raspberry, huckleberry and blueberry bushes choke the slope. Just five minutes farther downhill you have an even better view of the stream as it drops through the forest. Stave Lake glimmers below. In the sunlight of a late summer day the water in the lake is decidedly turquoise. The colour is the result of very fine sedimentation in the water, so fine that its reflection approaches the wavelength of visible light. Earlier in the summer the particles washing into the lake from winter snowmelt are larger, resulting in cloudier hues. Old stumps dot the surface of the lake's west side; the eastern side is littered with driftwood. High water levels at other times of the year would make landing on these shores tricky or even treacherous when strong winds toss all that debris about.

11 | RUSKIN AND ENVIRONS

BOATING ◄
CYCLING ◄
DRIVING ◄
FISHING ◄
NATURE OBSERVATION ◄
PADDLING ◄
PICNICKING ◄
SIGHTSEEING ◄
SWIMMING ◄
WALKING ◄

There are four recreation sites along the Stave River and at Hayward and Stave lakes. Set on the north side of Lougheed Highway (Highway 7) at the town of Ruskin, 30 mi. (50 km) east of Vancouver, each is worth a visit. Turn off the Lougheed at the sign to Rolley Lake Provincial Park to find them.

RUSKIN RECREATION AREA   Along the road to Rolley Lake you will pass the Ruskin dam, completed in 1930, the last of three hydroelectric dams in the Alouette-Stave-Ruskin project built by B.C. Hydro. Water from Alouette Lake is diverted half a mile (about 1 km) east through an underground tunnel to Stave Lake. Then lake water runs through the nearby Stave Falls and Blind Slough powerhouses and into Hayward Lake, where it generates even more power passing through the Ruskin powerhouse into the Stave River. The Ruskin dam provides power at peak periods when demand rises in the Lower Mainland. As a result, water levels in the river can change without warning, though B.C. Hydro does try to control water flow so that important spawning grounds in the gravel beds below the dam are not disturbed.

Coho and chum salmon run the river in late October and November, a good time for visiting and viewing. Wide spawning channels have been dug on each side of the river. The best viewing is had at the Ruskin Recreation Area, where the attractions are fishing, boating, picnicking and sightseeing (no camping or fires permitted). To reach it, take Ruskin Road across the top of the dam and descend 0.6 mi. (1 km) down the east side to the site gates. The boat launch (also gated) is on your left as you enter. Several picnic tables are located on a benchland above the Stave River. A short trail descends to the river, with a bridge crossing the spawning channel and leading out onto the banks of the river itself. Looking upstream you can see the dam, 194 ft. (59 m) high and 371 ft. (113 m) long. It's by far the most powerful of the three generating plants in the system, with a total capacity of 105,600 kw. Downstream from the recreation site you can see Ruskin and the wide expanse of the Fraser River.

HAYWARD LAKE RESERVOIR   Above the Hayward dam is the Hayward Lake Reservoir recreation area. The Railway trail, which follows an old railbed, runs the entire 3.7-mi. (6-km) length of Hayward Lake's west side to the recreation site at North Beach. Access is from one of three locations, two of them quite close together at the lake's south end. As you drive up Wilson Road past the dam, watch for parking signs. A steep staircase descends from the parking lot to the lake, so if you are planning to explore on bicycle you should park at the foot of Wilson Road next to the gated entrance to Railway trail. If there is no room there you'll have to use the parking area and carry your bike down.

Railway trail is wide and hard-packed as it runs beside Hayward Lake's south end. A small beach and outhouses are located 0.6 mi. (1 km) north of the trailhead. All along the way you will pass signs of the old trestle bridges that once carried track.

North of the beach the trail curves inland around a small inlet, rising and falling along a route that has been upgraded with new boardwalks and bridges to help visitors around the shore-line. This trail is very pretty where it enters a stand of old growth that was left when loggers took the rest of the cedar between 1890 and 1930; perhaps these trees were too young to cut at the time.

The feeling in the hushed cedar grove is one of intense green, with branches high above sheltering visitors who pass by on the forest floor below. Unfortunately, the experience is all too short-lived. As you make your way north the trail comes out beside the lake once more, narrowing abruptly as it does so. You can feel the old railway ties buried beneath your feet. Their spacing determines the cadence of your step; if you've ever walked a railway bed before, this will suddenly feel very familiar.

Stump-filled bays beside the trail define much of the appear-

Fishing the Stave River below the Ruskin dam

ance of Hayward Lake along the way to North Beach. It's quite obviously a flooded valley. A debris boom in front of the Hayward dam keeps loose driftwood from entering the intake shafts. It will take you an easy hour to walk the trail to North Beach, half that by bicycle. There are a few rough sections where the trail momentarily leads away from the lake through the forest. Several small bridges are noticeably in need of repair. Waterproof footwear is helpful when negotiating parts of the trail in wet weather. Keep an eye out for an elderly couple who make a daily circuit of Railway trail.

STAVE LAKE AND NORTH BEACH   At the north end of Hayward Lake, reached by driving up Wilson Road to Dewdney Trunk Road and proceeding east to the small settlement of Stave Falls (a community of a hundred homes at the time of the dams' construction), are two more recreation sites. One is a boat launch on Stave Lake; the other is the recreation area at North Beach on Hayward Lake. The two lakes are separated by the Stave dam.

North Beach is dotted with picnic tables and is a busy place in good weather. At other times it can be so deserted that it's almost spooky. As at Buntzen Lake—a B.C. Hydro recreation area east of Indian Arm—only hand-powered boats or boats with electric motors are permitted on Hayward Lake. (Canoe rentals are available on a seasonal basis from Clarks Estate

General Store in Stave Falls.) Larger, more powerful boats should launch on Stave Lake at a site 0.6 mi. (1 km) north of the North Beach turnoff.

As you enter the North Beach recreation area you will see the beach and picnic area just beyond the parking lot. The boat launch for Hayward Lake is just beside the parking lot and has its own driveway down to the lake. Although a paddle on the lake can be enjoyable, there are almost no places along the shoreline to stop.

A charming gazebo graces the grass lawns surrounding the beach. The history of the Stave dam project is depicted in archival photographs at an interpretive display nearby. If you're in the mood for a short walk, take the Pond circle trail to a bluff overlooking the reservoir. The trail begins at the south end of the beach, where the north end of the Railway trail is also located.

STAVE FALLS TO MISSION   If you cross the Stave Lake dam you'll find the road winds its way for 6 mi. (10 km) southeast towards Mission, passing through the small settlement of Steelhead along the way. Set back off the road around Steelhead are farms bearing the unmistakable imprint of the 1960s "back to the land" movement, side by side with newer developments. The hills beside the road are rich in gravel, as evidenced by a series of quarries you pass as you approach Mission's northern limits. Watch for a lovely Ukrainian Orthodox church built of cedar logs and shakes as you approach the Dewdney Trunk Road.

12 | MISSION AND ENVIRONS

Imagine being lucky enough to live on a ridge on the north side of the mighty Fraser River, overlooking the Matsqui Prairie, with towering Mount Baker as the centrepiece of your view. Residents of Mission enjoy this natural spectacle every day, weather permitting. You can, too, when you make a visit to Westminster Abbey, any of several well-kept parks or, best of all, hidden Ferncliff Gardens. There's also much to choose from close to Mission, including a drive to Cascade Falls Regional Park (built with access for the handicapped in mind) or a cycle tour of Nicomen Island.

Finding your way is not difficult. Take Lougheed Highway (Highway 7) east to Mission, 50 mi. (80 km) from Vancouver. Watch for the Travel Info Centre, located on the north side of the highway just past Mary Street, where you can obtain a Mission Visitors Guide with detailed street maps of the area.

FRASER RIVER HERITAGE PARK   Located at an important geographical point where the Fraser River makes an elbow turn on its way to the Pacific, Mission is tied historically to the Cariboo gold rush of the 1850s, but with a slightly different twist. With the influx of tens of thousands of miners pursuing gold came grief for the First Nations people through whose lands the prospectors travelled. In 1860 Father Fouquet, a French priest with the Oblates of Mary Immaculate, founded St. Mary's Mission to provide shelter, counselling and schooling for native people. It was the first and largest residential school of its kind in the Pacific Northwest. In 1959, the federal government rebuilt the school 1.8 mi. (3 km) east of the old site. Each year in July the Mission Powwow draws participants and spectators to a three-day festival of native singing, drumming and dancing held on the grounds of the new school, off the Lougheed Highway just east of the Travel Info Centre.

The remains of the old mission were cleared in 1965, and in its place is the expansive Fraser River Heritage Park. You can still see footprints of the old buildings near the bandshell. On the east side of the park is a small cemetery surrounded by a grove of tall, sturdy hemlocks. Father Fouquet is buried here in a section set aside for Oblate monks.

To find Fraser River Heritage Park, turn north off the Lougheed Highway on Third Avenue at its convergence with Mary Street. The park entrance is at Mary and Fifth. A log chalet, the Norma Kenney House, is located at the park entrance. It serves as a reception centre as well as being home to the Blackberry Kitchen, a good place to pause for refreshment in summer, and the Valley Treasures gift shop, which features work by local craftspeople.

Fraser River Heritage Park is also home to the annual Mission Folk Festival. One look at its wide-open spaces and you can easily imagine tents and sound stages dotting the grounds. In hot weather there is a cool ravine to visit in the shade of an adjacent forest. Trails lead off through the woods, linking the park with nearby neighbourhoods. No matter where you wander through the park, the views to the south are its most enthralling aspect.

WESTMINSTER ABBEY   On a nearby hillside stands Westminster Abbey, home to a Benedictine monastery. To find your way to the abbey from the Lougheed Highway as it passes through Mission, take Stave Lake Road to Dewdney Trunk Road. Turn right and go east along Dewdney. Watch for the abbey on your right just past the intersection of Dewdney and Goundrey Street.

Completed in 1982, Westminster Abbey stands atop a ridge overlooking the Fraser River Valley. Treat yourself to a visit for the view—even better than at Fraser River Heritage Park—and a choral vespers service in the abbey. The simplicity of the unaccompanied chanting stands in remarkable contrast to the imposing character of the abbey itself, designed by Vancouver architect Asbjorn Gathe. In late afternoon, when the slanting rays

Westminster Abbey bell tower

of the sun make their way through the modern stained-glass windows, the abbey's interior is bathed in shades of burnt orange and cool blues, highlighting a series of 21 bas-reliefs mounted on the walls. An interpretive description of the panels, available from the information office (next to the abbey's main entrance), will help you assign meaning to each of the scenes depicted in storybook fashion. Visiting hours at the monastery, where the ancient Benedictine credo has always been to show hospitality to guests of all faiths, are weekday afternoons from 1:30 to 4:30, and 2 to 4 on Sundays. The 30-minute vespers service begins at 5:30 on weekdays and 4:30 on Sundays.

If you are here just to visit the grounds, formerly a family farm and still operated by the self-sufficient monks, make your way along the path that leads south from the abbey's parking lot. It makes a gently winding approach to one of the most commanding viewpoints found anywhere in the Fraser Valley, a must-see for visitors. Large knolls thrust up from the valley floor to the east; the well-ordered Matsqui Prairie lies before you to the south, across the mighty Fraser from the agricultural lands of Hatzic and Nicomen Island, surmounted by Sumas and Baker mountains.

FERNCLIFF GARDENS   At certain times of the year, from the abbey viewpoint you can see a small but intense patch of colour on the eastern slopes below: Ferncliff Gardens. After the tulips and daffodils have finished blooming in the nearby Bradner region, nature goes into a bit of a lull. But not for long. Across the river, Ferncliff Gardens provides one of the most beautiful floral displays in the valley, especially from May to October. Not only is the variety of blooms awesome to see, but the setting is second to none.

Ferncliff Gardens was started in 1920 in Hatzic, which is 1.8 mi. (3 km) east of Mission. Once a thriving commercial berry-growing centre, Hatzic today more closely resembles a bedroom community. Signs of redevelopment are already everywhere around Ferncliff, and as the years go by it will become even more of an oasis.

To find the gardens, turn north onto the Dewdney Trunk Road at the Hatzic Esso station, drive three blocks, then turn right on Henry Street. Continue down Henry to its end where it turns into McTaggart Street (which becomes a dirt lane), then turn right at the Ferncliff Gardens sign. A lovely Tudor-style farmhouse sits sheltered behind a cedar hedge; the main barn and garden office lie just beyond at road's end.

Specializing in irises, peonies and dahlias, current owner David Jack has an open-door policy for visitors, who are invited to drop in anytime. Easily more than a hundred varieties of irises and nearly that many peonies bathe the landscape with a spectrum of brilliant hues in May and June. Flowering continues, row upon row, until the end of June, then the fields lie fallow for a short while before acres of dahlia blossoms open between early August and mid-October. During these times many gardeners visit Ferncliff to make their selections. When blossoming finishes the bulbs, tubers and rhizomes are harvested and shipped out to buyers. The challenge faced by anyone who visits here is to come away without dreaming—in Technicolor, of course—of creating their own backyard Ferncliff. For more information on Ferncliff, contact David Jack, 8394 McTaggart Street, S.S. 1, Mission V2V 6S6, 826-2447.

HATZIC AND NEILSON PARKS   Photographers will enjoy the views of Ferncliff from the open slopes of nearby Hatzic Park (its entrance is off Draper Street). This is also a good place to picnic after a visit to the gardens. Another spot suited to this same purpose is nearby Neilson Regional Park, located on the west side of Hatzic Lake and an easy five-minute drive from Ferncliff. Just drive north from the gardens on McTaggart, turn left on McEwen, then immediately right on Edwards Street, and follow the signs to the park from here. Open fields slope down to the shore of Hatzic Lake from the parking lot. There are numerous picnic tables, a swimming beach and a salmon spawning channel on Draper Creek that teems with activity come October. (Unfortunately, no domestic pets are allowed in Neilson park.) You can launch a hand-carried boat here and spend some leisure time exploring Hatzic Lake. From out on the water Westminster Abbey's bell tower appears on the skyline above the park.

CASCADE FALLS REGIONAL PARK   For an extensive look at the region around Mission, drive a short distance east of Hatzic Lake on the Lougheed Highway to Sylvester Road and turn left. The rural setting along the road makes for a pleasant drive north as you head towards Stave Lake through the Hatzic Prairie and Miracle Valley. This is definitely backwoods country; suddenly the hustle and bustle of the Fraser Valley seem distant. You may not wish to drive the entire 21 mi. (35 km) to Stave Lake—access to the lake is better from the boat launch at Stave Falls—but 9 mi. (15 km) along is the Cascade Falls park, a satisfying enough destination, and 3 mi. (5 km) farther north is secluded Davis Lake Provincial Park, best suited to fishing.

At Cascade Falls Regional Park, wide trails and a foot bridge allow everyone an approach to the soothing waterfall where visitors receive an ear massage from the music of its tumbling passage. A deep resonance emanates from the waterfall as it drops into a pool at its base, detectably vibrating the rocky hillside. Split logs serve as both benches and picnic tables. In wet months the water in Cascade Creek runs at full bore, first dropping through a narrow chute at the top of the falls into a large catchpool, then another long drop to the valley floor, a total of 164 ft. (50 m) in all. The only thing that may detract from your enjoyment is the sight of the clearcut tops of the surrounding mountains. A dike trail runs along Cascade Creek as it flows west of the falls into Stave Lake. Much of the land on which the dike is built is private, but there are opportunities for cycling in places.

NICOMEN ISLAND   An even better venue for cycling is a short distance farther east of Hatzic on level-surfaced Nicomen Island. Entirely rural, this countryside is as sleepy as it gets out here in the Fraser Valley. After the Lougheed Highway passes Hatzic Lake, it runs through the small town of Dewdney and then crosses a bridge onto Nicomen Island. (Just before the bridge, River Road leads off to the right and follows the shoreline of Nicomen Slough past a pub and a number of wharves to Dewdney Nature Park, where there's a boat launch.) You may wish to leave your vehicle beside the bridge at Dewdney and use your bicycle to explore the lengthy dike trails around the perimeter of Nicomen Island as far east as the rustic town of Deroche, located where Highway 7 crosses from Nicomen back onto the mainland.

13 | BRADNER/ MOUNT LEHMAN

In the gently rolling hills east of Vancouver the vernal equinox signals the start of a festive season. Everyone keeps one eye out for the first robin, the other for the first daffodil. Both are harbingers of winter's true end. Whether you're in a celebratory mood, looking to shake off cabin fever after a winter indoors or just looking for an opportunity to dig your bicycle out of the garage, the Bradner and Mount Lehman region has a welcome ready for you. Even if the spring breeze still has a chill edge to it, pack a lunch, as there are sheltered spots beside the nearby Fraser River for picnicking. If you time your arrival close to the Easter weekend, plan to attend the Bradner Daffodil Festival, held here annually since 1928.

To get to Bradner, take Highway 1 east to the exit at 264th Street, just past the exit to Fort Langley. After swinging north on 264th as it crosses the Trans-Canada, turn immediately east on 56th Avenue (Interprovincial Way) to Bradner Road. Turn right here. Cross the railway tracks, and watch for the Bradner Community Hall on the west side of the road next to the school. The daffodil festival is held here, complete with its legendary bake sale. The small park across the road from the Bradner General Store, complete with a gazebo, is one potential picnic location.

On another spring day in 1906, an English gardener, recently arrived in Vancouver, spotted a stump full of blooming daffodils. Fenwick Fatkin instantly knew that he'd found his calling in the New World. He bought property in Bradner, a small farming town in the Fraser valley, and set about cultivating

The Fraser River from Albion

several varieties of this popular member of the amaryllis family. In 1928, Fatkin held a "parlour show" in his home, featuring 14 varieties of daffs. Seeking to increase his selection, he enlisted the aid of one of Holland's leading bulb suppliers, Wilhelmus Vander Zalm, Sr. Vander Zalm later found himself stranded in Canada during a 1940 visit because the Nazis had invaded Holland. When the war ended, Fatkin sponsored the entry of the rest of the Vander Zalm family, including Wilhelmus's wife, Agatha, and their two daughters and four sons (one of whom, Wilhelmus Jr.—better known as Bill—would become premier of the province).

These days more than 400 varieties of daffodils bloom in the area's fields. At this time of year, the sight of daffodils and narcissi poking their yellow or white heads above the ditches is your first clue that you're close to tiny Bradner, a town so far off the beaten path that visitors might otherwise miss it entirely. You'll soon start to come across small roadside stands with bunches of daffodils for sale. Many of the stands operate on the honour system: just choose your daffs and leave your money.

Many back roads crisscross this plateau atop the Pemberton Hills bordering the Fraser River. No matter what your vantage point, you'll find yourself lifting your eyes north to one of the best full-face views of the Golden Ears and south to broad, glaciated Mount Baker. As you drive east or west of Bradner, you drop down into prairie land, with Fort Langley to the west and Matsqui to the east.

The area around Bradner is perfect for either a leisurely inspection by car or an energetic bicycle ride. Many of the roads on the plateau are flat, and traffic is generally light. One caution: the shoulders of most roads are narrow and lined with shallow drainage ditches. This does not allow much room for Fido to run, should you bring along the family pet.

If you drive out with bikes on board and are wondering where to leave your car, try the large parking area beside the Bradner schoolhouse or a second one at the north end of Bradner Road beside Jubilee Hall, several miles north of town. Just behind the hall the pavement narrows, then becomes gravel for an exciting descent on the Langley side into the valley below. Travelling north from Bradner to Jubilee you'll pass well-kept homes, some with daffodils for sale in spring. One farm in particular has hundreds of daffodils under cultivation. The owners here welcome visitors and encourage them to walk back out into the field for a closer look at the many variations in their colouring and form.

Around Bradner are a dozen roads to choose from, most of which feed into each other at one point or other. You'll spot an occasional heritage marker to help direct you to some interesting vistas, but otherwise finding your way around this small region can be rather haphazard.

A century ago, riverboats served the fledgling community of nearby Mount Lehman, an early port of entry to Matsqui, bringing produce from local farms to the city dwellers of New Westminster. By 1908, the B.C. Electric Company railway had laid tracks alongside this stretch of the Fraser River (the route was later taken over by Canadian National Railways). In 1992, as part of Matsqui's centennial celebrations, the Landing Road Heritage Trail was one of several revitalized. Not long, it leads down through the forest to an old railway siding and log pilings beside the Fraser, reminders of earlier times. Several picnic tables are set beside the trail. Follow the roadside markers east of Jubilee Hall to reach the Landing Road Heritage Trail. There's plenty of parking beside a fragrant hog farm at road's end.

Harris Road leads east of Mount Lehman and links up with

The last remnants of Mount Lehman's river heritage

the Matsqui trail. This dike trail was once part of a route from Horseshoe Bay to Hope. Now a Greater Vancouver Regional District park, it extends a level 5 mi. (8 km) along the dike, past the Mission Bridge and open fields with grazing cattle to the slopes of Sumas Mountain. If you'd like to ride farther, carry on here, where there is also good picnicking beside the Fraser River.

14 | ALDERGROVE LAKE REGIONAL PARK

CYCLING ◄
DRIVING ◄
PICNICKING ◄
SWIMMING ◄
VIEWPOINTS ◄
WALKING ◄
X-C SKIING ◄

Here's a little park that's well worth including as part of an outing in the Langley-Matsqui districts. For one season of the year—summer—Aldergrove Lake is a magnet for overheated kids on vacation. The rest of the year, it's a quiet corner in the country interlaced with a trail that loops back on itself in three places as it passes through a densely wooded forest. You can walk, ride or even cross-country ski these trails when conditions are right.

To drive to Aldergrove Lake park take the Trans-Canada Highway east to the 264th Street exit, head south to 8th Avenue (Huntington Road), then turn east to reach the main park entrance at the intersection of 8th Avenue and 272nd Street. (There are equestrian and pedestrian entrances on the west and east sides of the park, 272nd Street and Lefeuvre Road, respectively.)

Alternatively, you can avoid the high-speed pressure of the Trans-Canada and explore the region at your leisure if you make your way to and from the park by following the Langley back roads south of the Fraser Highway. The drive out along the country roads of Surrey and Langley is a reward in itself. In autumn, the harvest from nearby fields fills front porches and roadside stands to the brim with colourful Turk's Turban, butternut, Delicato, acorn and Hubbard squashes and mound upon mound of pumpkins. Follow the Fraser Highway east of Langley, picking your way along sections of Old Yale Road (where you can still find it), especially in the Murrayville area around 216th and 232nd streets. A dilapidated automotive garage, a

View from Aldergrove Lake trail

faded pie shop and a homestead covered in a collection of
weathervanes are rewarding sights for following your nose on
your way to the lake.

The countryside around Aldergrove Lake hasn't quite felt the
impact of the urbanization seen in many other parts of Langley.
Little creeks crisscross the fields, culverted under roadways and
bridged where they really display their girth. Salmon spawn in
some, especially when the creeks are running high after a recent
rainstorm. In the autumn quiet there's the occasional sound of
salmon thrashing and slapping the water in their drive to reach
a spawning bed.

If you pull into the park with high hopes that water levels in
Aldergrove Lake have benefited from rainstorms too—after all,
Pepin Creek flows through the park on its way south into nearby
Whatcom County—think again. Imagine an enormous bathtub
with the plug pulled: this is Aldergrove Lake in the off-season
from Labour Day to Victoria Day. Entirely manmade, shaped
like a dirt racing oval with a concrete pad on its bottom, the
lake can be bone dry. The size of the parking lot tells you that
the lake is very popular in summer, but most times the lot is as

empty as the basin. Nearby is a large playing field and the Blacktail group picnic area with a covered barbecue shelter (you can reserve this by calling 432-6352).

Don't think the worst if you arrive to find the lake empty: there's more to Aldergrove Lake Park than first meets the eye. You can always walk or ride your bicycle on the extensive park trails. Take care not to spook any horses you may encounter; slow down when approaching them and stand aside on the down side of the trail while they pass. Campbell Valley, another regional park farther west in Langley, has a landscape much like Aldergrove Lake's, but bicycling isn't permitted there.

You won't need any prompting to mount up on a bicycle and head south along an easy-going series of trails through the sheltering forest. The farther you ride, the better it gets. Then the forest opens up and you're riding over hills beside farmland where berry bushes colour the horizon. Continue up and down, back and forth, until you find a little park bench installed on a knoll, from which the view is of Mount Baker's snowcone, weather permitting. At sunset you can watch it turn shades of pink and red in the setting sun.

A massive erratic boulder, a leftover from glacial times, is nestled in the woods near Lefeuvre Road where the trail heads north from the bench. The Transformer, a supernatural character from native mythology who went about changing animate beings into inanimate objects, must have had a hand in this one. (A transformation of another kind has influenced the Hunt Bridge, located close to the pedestrian entrance on 272nd Street: the recycled timbers used in its construction came from Vancouver's old Cambie Street Bridge in 1985.)

Aldergrove Lake's trails are suited to beginner and intermediate-level bicycle riders who like to enjoy a view and a challenge at the same time. There's nothing extreme about these routes. By the end of a long looping ride you may have covered only half the distance possible on the trails that lazily circle through the park. As you pack up, share again the amazement that your expectations have once more been exceeded. Aldergrove Lake may have been dry, but your initial misgivings will have vaporized by the time you head home, floating on a cloud of fulfilment.

15 | SASQUATCH PROVINCIAL PARK

BOATING ◄
CAMPING ◄
CYCLING ◄
DRIVING ◄
FISHING ◄
PADDLING ◄
PICNICKING ◄
SWIMMING ◄
WALKING ◄

Sasquatch Provincial Park first opened to the public in May 1968. Since then the three campgrounds situated beside two of the four lakes within the park have drawn visitors from throughout the Lower Mainland. The park has room for plenty of campers at the 177 sites, and there's enough recreational diversity spread over its 3013 acres (1220 ha) to satisfy the choosiest of day trippers. When visitors fill the park, the Bench Campground, an overflow area on the table of land slightly above Lakeside Campground at Deer Lake, is opened, providing 65 additional vehicle sites. But unless you arrive early enough to beat the long-weekend crowds between Victoria Day and Labour Day, your chances of finding any campsite, let alone much in the way of tranquillity, are slim. In order to truly revel in the natural atmosphere of Sasquatch Park, practise contrary thinking: head there on the Monday of a holiday weekend when the crowds are on their way home.

Sasquatch Provincial Park is on the east side of Harrison Lake 84 mi. (135 km) east of Vancouver and 3.7 mi. (6 km) north of Harrison Hot Springs, and is accessible from either the Trans-Canada or Highway 7.

At the entrance to the park is the grassy Green Point picnic area, spread beside the shores of Harrison Lake, which features dozens of wooden tables stained honey gold, many with barbecues, an open play area and a beach with great exposure to the afternoon sun. This is important—the waters of Harrison Lake, a deep fiord, are cold year-round.

East of Green Point the road turns from pavement to gravel

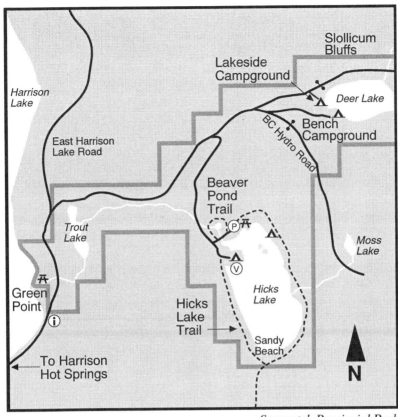

Sasquatch Provincial Park

as it passes beside small Trout Lake, entirely surrounded by thick green growth. Access is limited to packed-in boats and there is no beach.

About 2 mi. (3 km) farther east the park road divides, with one branch leading 1.2 mi. (2 km) south to Hicks Lake, or the same distance east to Deer Lake. The use of a campsite at either lake, with plenty of dry red cedar firewood and drinking water available, costs about $10 per night. Gates restrict motorized vehicles to the main road, but several old logging roads leading off through the park are perfectly suited for exploration by bicycle.

If you have time at your disposal, check out both Hicks and Deer lakes. Deer Lake is the smaller of the two. Judging from the old stumps that still populate the forest, Sasquatch Park was logged many years ago. Today the sheltering forest is more deciduous than evergreen. From spring through early fall bird songs fill the air and mingle with a chorus of frogs until late evening. The road to the lakes climbs through a saddle in the slope of the modest-sized mountains surrounding Harrison Lake, where the Cascade and Coast ranges merge. One of the most arresting sights looking west from Deer Lake is a new moon hanging in the saddle as the sky darkens. Watch too for the sight of mountain goats in the early morning light on the slopes of Slollicum Bluffs, which rise above the lake's north side.

Deer Lake is a rather simple body of water with little hidden from the eye from a vantage point on the beach at its western end. There's a children's play area just uphill from lakeside with slides and a jungle-gym setup. Only quiet electric motors are allowed on boats that put in here, whereas on nearby Hicks Lake gas-driven motors up to 10 horsepower can be used. Other than on long weekends, visitors with small boats will usually have the lakes to themselves. You can launch from the beach, where in the morning the aromas of smoke and fresh coffee are carried on the breeze from nearby campsites, or you can drive your car down to a small dock tethered at the south end of the beach.

The circumference of Deer Lake can be easily paddled in an hour without rushing. From the beach you can also walk a lakeside trail out to a sandy point where fishing and swimming may suit your mood. Or you can cycle the fire and service roads that run well back into the mountains surrounding Deer Lake. For those who wish to get away from the beaches beside the campgrounds, there are more isolated sandy stretches that can be reached by boat at the far end of either lake.

Paddle quietly around Deer Lake, perhaps stalking an eagle sitting on a logjam where the lake drains off into a green marsh, while an osprey floating above spies its breakfast in the clear waters on which you float. Looking at the slopes thick with broad-leafed maple, white birch and poplar in summer, you can imagine how alluring a sight this will be in autumn when the leaves change colour.

You could spend a morning on Deer Lake, then explore nearby Hicks Lake, 2.5 mi. (4 km) away and twice as large. It's not as open as Deer Lake, with several points of land jutting out into the lake from which to fish or catch a view of the Cascade mountains rising on the southern horizon. As you approach Hicks you'll see signs pointing in several different directions.

You should decide whether you want to head over to the day-use parking lot next to a boat launch and picnic area, or proceed to the campground, where there is also a beach and picnic area. Trails link all the areas together and it's only a few minutes' walk between the day-use area and the campground. However, when you're packing coolers and beach equipment, you don't want to lug it too far from the car. For the best views, check out the beach beside the campground amphitheatre: the peaks of the Skagit Range near Chilliwack Lake stand out on the southern horizon. There are also some good fishing spots here on a point of land in front of campsites 2 to 17 (some of the most desirable locations, along with sites 36 to 41).

For a short but nonetheless interesting walk, check out the Beaver Pond trail, which leads around a marshy area near the day parking lot. Boardwalks and bridges take you past the small creek flowing west from Hicks Lake, part of which has been diverted by a beaver dam into a small pond. (The creek flows next into Trout Lake and eventually finds its way into Harrison.)

Put your boat in at the Hicks Lake launch site, or walk the trail ringing the lake to Sandy Beach at the south end, perhaps targeting it as your picnic destination if you're travelling light. You'll reach the beach in an hour after a stroll in the shade along an old logging road. Partway around is the group campsite, in front of which is a good beach. An easy swim offshore are two small forested islands, perfectly sized for adventure exploration with children and a good place to cast in a fishing line. Rainbow trout thrive in these waters, as the osprey and eagles can attest.

On weekdays you may well have Sandy Beach entirely to yourself and may have passed no one aside from a group of seniors on a day outing as you walk the trail. Like yourselves, they've indulged in a little commonsense contrary thinking to beat the crowds. When everyone else is headed one way, try going in the opposite direction. It may mean rearranging your work or holiday schedule, but you'll find the rewards are embarrassingly rich.

16 | CULTUS LAKE

Mention Cultus Lake to many people and what immediately comes to mind is images of speed boats, summer parties, water slides and, above all, crowds of campers. While this is pretty much the case during the hottest days of summer, there is a quieter side to the lake and its environs at most other seasons. Even in July and August it's possible to have a pleasant visit at this large, warm lake nestled in the folds of the Cascade Mountains in the south Fraser Valley just 60 mi. (100 km) east of Vancouver.

To reach Cultus Lake, follow Highway 1 for 55 mi. (90 km) almost to Chilliwack. Watch for signs indicating the exit to Yarrow and the parks at Cultus and Chilliwack lakes. Once you've made the exit you are on No. 3 Road. As you travel through the Fraser Valley farmland you'll see many fruit and vegetable stands at roadside, along with signs advertising eggs or honey posted at the entrances to some homes. The town of Yarrow, located on a section of the Old Yale Road, is a slice of B.C. heritage. Just south of here the road crosses the Chilliwack-Vedder River, then divides, with one section heading south to Cultus Lake and the other leading east beside the river to Chilliwack Lake. Cultus Lake is 2.5 mi. (4 km) from this point.

According to *British Columbia Place Names* (G.P.V. and Helen B. Akrigg, Sono Nis Press, 1992), the local Indians once believed that supernatural creatures lived in the lake and manifested themselves as dirty swirlings in the water. These days you could be excused for thinking that the name is a direct reference to the jet-skiers who buzz around the shoreline, whipping the

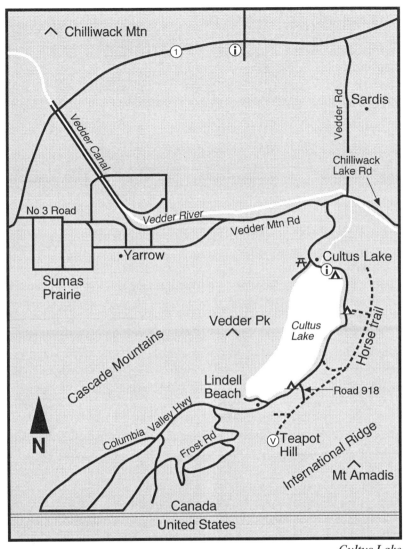

Cultus Lake

waters into a frenzy. The natives called the lake Tso-wallie; the modern name comes from a Chinook word meaning "worthless" or "bad," perhaps because of a native taboo or in reference to the squall-plagued waters.

Cultus Lake has limited drainage aside from the Sweltzer River, which flows out the north end. A small creek enters at the south end, but otherwise there is no source of fresh cold water to feed the lake once the snowpack has melted from the surrounding slopes. In comparison to the frigid waters of nearby Chilliwack and Harrison lakes, Cultus is a bathtub, which most surely accounts for the popularity it has sustained with visitors for the better part of this century. For this reason, too, fishing in the park is good, with rainbows, cutthroats and Dolly Varden. There are a number of working farms on the Columbia Valley benchland above the south end of the lake. No local roads cross the nearby Canada-U.S. border.

The original settlement at Cultus Lake was at its north end. There is still a small community of year-round residents here and another at Lindell Beach at the lake's south end, though most cottages are used only on a seasonal basis. Row upon row of small, well-kept cabins, built close together, now ring the shores at both ends of the lake.

CULTUS MUNICIPAL BEACH   Although much of the summer activity has expanded along the east side of the lake, it is here at Cultus's north end that you will find some of the best swimming, especially if you have smaller children in tow. There is a maze of docks, complete with a small slide, on which to sun while keeping an eye on young bathers. On the nearby lawns of the municipal park you'll find plenty of room to hold barbecues, with a picnic gazebo, tennis courts and washroom facilities close at hand. Beach Buoy Leisure Rentals (858-8841), housed in an old wood-frame building set back above the water, rents out canoes, rowboats and paddlewheelers.

To reach the municipal beach, turn right at the large wooden public parking sign as you enter the town of Cultus Lake and drive the short distance to lakeside. Even if your destination is the nearby provincial park this is an interesting location through which to stroll and admire the cottages. Some sport names—"Bide-a-wee," "Laffalot," "Dunroamin"—and mounted atop one beachfront cabin are several pairs of ancient homemade water-skis equipped with cut-off rubber boots, signs of earlier, more ingenious times.

CULTUS LAKE PROVINCIAL PARK   Back on the main highway, once you've past the mall, the go-kart track, the commercial water slides and the stable where trail rides may be arranged, Columbia Valley Highway, the main road around the lake, heads south for

Municipal dock at north end of Cultus Lake, with International Ridge in the distance

2.5 mi. (4 km) towards the provincial park. Along the way it passes the well-kept Sunnyside Campground (858-3324), one of several acceptable commercial options should you find all the public campsites in the park already taken. Just past here on the east side of the road is the park headquarters (858-7161), where well-informed staff can answer questions on recreational options in the surrounding district.

There are four campgrounds within the park, as well as three large picnic grounds. During summer months the gatehouse at the entrance to the park is open 24 hours a day. If you are seeking camping space this is the place to register. An overnight camping fee (about $15) is charged from April to Thanksgiving weekend in October.

The only campground that is actually beside the water (other than the group campground at Honeymoon Bay, which can be reserved for nonprofit youth-oriented groups) is Delta Grove, where there are 58 units, including six double units. Of these, 18 sites are beside the lake, many with their own small section of beach. The other three campgrounds at Entrance Bay (52 campsites including five doubles) Clear Creek (80 campsites) and Maple Bay (106 campsites including nine doubles) are set

95

back a short distance above the lake. All campgrounds and picnic areas have very clean facilities, though the amount of hot water for showering varies depending on the time of day and the number of visitors competing for it. Firewood is supplied. Both Entrance Bay and Maple Bay have a boat launch, beach and picnic day-use area.

The boundaries of the park encompass both sides of Cultus Lake, but only the southeast side is developed for recreation. To the northwest is open countryside where second-growth forest is beginning to establish itself. Much of the northwest side of the lake is made inaccessible by cliffs that plummet to the water's edge.

Steep International Ridge rises above the campsites and day-use areas on the southeast side of the lake. Several trails traverse the ridge. One particularly popular one leads to a viewpoint on Teapot Hill, named by two surveyors in the early 1950s. While laying out boundaries for the new park, whose 1625 acres (658 ha) were officially opened to the public in February 1948, they found an abandoned teapot on the open face of the knoll that rises 2460 ft. (750 m) above the lake, affording good views to the south, west and north.

Of the several approaches to Teapot Hill, the easiest begins on the east side of the road between Delta Grove and Honeymoon Bay. The entrance is marked by a gate and signposts. One sign reads "Road 918"; its companion points the way uphill to Teapot Hill. There is limited parking next to the trailhead. Interpretive signs are situated at various places along wide, well-worn Road 918. Near the top the road forks right while the well-marked trail to Teapot Hill leads uphill to the left. The forest through which the road and trail runs is made up largely of second-growth western hemlock and tall broadleaf maple. In autumn, as the maple leaves turn golden with the change in seasons, the forest around Cultus Lake is bright and colourful, with the rich smell and crisp sound of dry leaves crunching underfoot as you walk along. Total walking time one way from the road to the top of Teapot Hill is less than an hour.

From the top, the most interesting views are of Lindell Beach and south to the Columbia Valley, which opens and then narrows its way into the United States, with several peaks of the Cascade Mountains rising in the distance.

A horse trail runs much of the way along International Ridge.

It joins Road 918 near Honeymoon Bay. Feeder trails lead from both the Entrance Bay and Clear Creek campgrounds to the horse trail, providing a pleasant alternative to the more straightforward approach to Teapot Hill via Road 918 mentioned above. The walk one way from Entrance Bay to Teapot Hill is less than two hours: from Clear Creek it's 90 minutes one way. The horse trail offers more variety than Road 918, as it rises and falls along the hillside below International Ridge.

One sight that's always a pleasure is the old moss-covered bridge spanning Teapot Creek, a 10-minute walk north of Road 918 on the horse trail. There are many signs of old logging roads in the forest, most of which have diminished over time to little more than a shadow of their original selves. One leads up the ridge beside Teapot Creek and is still in use by horse riders. It dead-ends after 30 minutes in a grove where, judging by the size of the nurse logs on the forest floor and one particularly large blasted stump, huge cedar trees once stood. Above this grove the sides of International Ridge become increasingly steep as they rise towards the razorback crest high above. The face of the ridge is lined with steep gullies; bushwacking between the Teapot Creek trail and Teapot Hill would be extremely laborious. (Although some maps of the area show a trail leading up onto International Ridge from the north end of the park, the park staff advise that this is a badly maintained, rough and rocky route that should not be attempted alone and is perhaps best avoided altogether.)

Throughout the summer months a nightly interpretive program is presented by members of the park staff at the Maple Bay amphitheatre. A list of topics and dates is posted at the information kiosks at each of the park campgrounds.

EXPLORING BEYOND CULTUS LAKE   The Columbia Valley Highway leads south from the park onto the benchland above the town of Lindell Beach. Lindell Beach is similar in flavour to the community at the north end of Cultus Lake and offers a variety of commercial services. From here you may choose to drive through the Columbia Valley, an enjoyable one-hour jaunt, or to explore the area by bicycle. In contrast to the narrow shoulders and highway traffic running the length of Cultus Lake, the roads south of Lindell Beach are far less busy, making them ideal for cycling.

Columbia Valley Highway divides shortly south of the golf

course. It really doesn't matter which of the two, Frost Road or Columbia Valley, you choose to follow, as one feeds into the other near the U.S. border, creating a loop through the valley. Along the way a variety of side roads lead off into the far reaches of the valley. Avoid any that are posted "No Exit" and you will have no trouble wending your way along.

Near the border on the valley's east side the waters of Frost Creek run towards Cultus Lake. Canyon Road is a pleasant, albeit narrow, gravel road that leads down to a bridge spanning the creek, then back up to Frost Road. Both major roads level out soon after cresting on the benchland above Lindell Beach and run 7.4 mi. (12 km) to the American border. The border is marked by one small obelisk and a narrow 40-foot (12-m) cut visible on the hillside above the valley. On the south side of a farm field straddling the border you can see the road that leads north from Maple Falls near Mount Baker but which does not cross the border or join up anywhere on the Canadian side. Viewed from here, the rolling countryside surrounding Cultus Lake is reminiscent of the scenery in the Okanagan Valley.

Several sites to watch for at roadside include a pony farm and Bertrand Creek Farms. The Jammy, Bertrand Creek's gift shop, sells Columbia Valley jams, jellies and spreads made from their own black, red and white currants, hazelnuts, blueberries, blackberries and raspberries, as well as the rarest of treats from the Prairies, Saskatoon berries. The Jammy is open daily.

FRASER RIVER ESTUARY |

WHERE THE RIVER
MEETS THE SEA

The Fraser River dominates the Lower Mainland with a quiet power. The fact that the force of its flow has been contained, channelled, bridged and diked in no way denigrates the river's magnificence. After coursing 850 mi. (1370 km) from its headwaters in the Rocky Mountains, it swells like a symphony to a crescendo on our doorstep.

Over the past half-century, as industry grew on the banks of the Fraser, recreational use diminished. Public access to the river shrank as the shoreline was gradually leased to companies who used the Fraser as a liquid road to carry their product to market or hold it in long lines of booms until needed on shore. From the Fraser's mouth on the Strait of Georgia and along its banks for 30 mi. (50 km) to Mission is a litter of industrial users, construction docks and more than 40 lumber mills. Recently, one of the river's last fishing bars, near Fort Langley, was leased to a lumber company for log booming.

In the mid-Seventies Environment Canada conducted a study of the Fraser River estuary. Its purpose was, as explained at the time by government naturalist Peggy Ward, "to develop a management plan for the Fraser estuary [that] will recognize the importance of the river to human activity and the need for preservation of its ecological integrity." Following the release of the study, the provincial and federal environment ministries signed an accord that set up the Fraser River Estuary Recreational Plan.

Each time I visit the Fraser I see more signs of how this plan is affecting public access to the river in positive ways, even though the quality of the water in the river itself is worse now

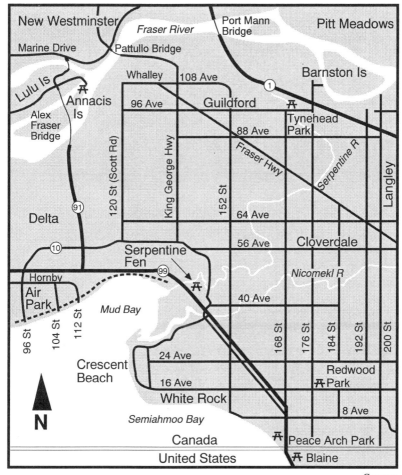

Surrey

than when the study was undertaken almost 20 years ago. You'll now find an increasing number of parks with riverside walkways and bicycle paths. Two major public markets front on the river, one in downtown New Westminster and the other at Bridgeport in Richmond, each with a marina. In addition, there are numerous places from which to launch a canoe or kayak for floating exploration.

Take advantage of these increased opportunities to adventure on or beside the river, and let the Fraser become your companion, your guide and your mentor. It's been running by our front door long enough to know a thing or two worth learning.

17 | TYNEHEAD REGIONAL PARK

PICNICKING ◄
NATURE OBSERVATION ◄
WALKING ◄

Tynehead Regional Park, home to the headwaters of the Serpentine River, is a sheltering place for wildlife in the midst of Surrey's housing boom. Now the park is also providing its newest neighbours sanctuary from the same plague faced by the area's fish, game and bird life: the overpowering forces of development. Hemmed in as it is by a major highway, it's a miracle that Tynehead can offer both serenity and quietude in its 642 acres (260 ha) of grassy meadows and second-growth cedar, hemlock, ash and maple.

Everything about Tynehead park comes as a surprise to first-time visitors. For one thing, it's quite easy to find. Simply take the exit south on 176th Street from the Trans-Canada and make the first turn west on 96th Avenue. From here you have a choice of two approaches. Either turn right at the next major intersection, 168th Street, and drive to the entrance at the road's north end, or continue west to the park entrance beside the Tynehead Hatchery.

Along 168th Street, empty fields roll off towards the west; a large section of the park lies to the east, undisturbed by development of any kind. Within minutes you'll be in the parking lot. You may have seen the information kiosk before from the Trans-Canada. A 10-minute walk from here, on a trail leading across the meadow and past some big cedars, you'll link up with the Serpentine Loop trail leading to the picnic area. There's nothing to stop you from heading off towards a quiet part of the park away from trails and roads. You can find a sheltered spot by the hedgerows if that suits your mood. Kids will enjoy

Trail through the Tynehead woods

getting down by the river to search for tadpoles, so bring rubber boots and a pail.

Along with the Nicomekl River, the Serpentine flows west into Mud Bay through the vastness of the Surrey flood plain. You cross it near the end of its journey to the sea as you drive along Highway 99 north of the Crescent Beach/White Rock exit. Its course twists back and forth on the map, and the thought of canoeing it—just to see where it goes—may have appealed to your adventurous spirit. But after one look at the section of the Serpentine that runs through Tynehead park, you'll know you wouldn't have made it this far upstream without a struggle. This is actually the headwaters of the river, fed by several creeks in the park and a natural spring. In springtime and after rainstorms, when the river runs faster than you might expect, high water cuts into the sandy banks, regularly bringing cedar and poplar trees crashing down across the river. These make good bridges for explorers during drier, warmer weather. High winds also contribute to the uprooting—if you visit on a gusty day, watch out for branches plummeting to the forest floor.

Several viewing platforms, well situated for birding, are perched above the river, as well as two small bridges that lead walkers across sections of the Serpentine. In most places the trail is hard-packed, suitable for wheelchairs and strollers. Close to the river, the forest is predominantly second-growth cedar and mature vine maple. Thick bramble bushes, matted down by snowfalls during parts of the year, skirt the cedars' low-lying branches, and a thin, hard layer of packed snow can persist on sheltered stretches of the trail long after a storm. Dried berries from each year's abundant crop help birds in the area survive these hard times.

Near the park's southern boundary where the Serpentine flows out of the park is the Tynehead Hatchery. Run by a volunteer organization, the Serpentine Enhancement Society, this is the site of a fish release each spring as part of the Salmonid Enhancement Program. (For information on the dates of the release, to which the public is invited, call 589-9127.) Come fall, you can see fish migrating to the spawning grounds in the park. As the Serpentine River becomes quite silty at times, a well has been drilled near the hatchery to provide a source of clean water for the fish tanks during the earliest stages of roe development.

The sound of the water in the river effectively camouflages the rumble of highway traffic. A profusion of cedar stumps throughout the park, some of them hollow, are reminders of the extensive grove that once stood here. Some stumps act as nurse logs, supporting as many as eight tall young hemlocks intent on taking their place in the sun.

Walk west of the Serpentine Loop trail to Picnic Hollow. Take the Trillium trail to a viewpoint of the Butterfly Garden, which has been specifically planted to attract members of this insect order. Well-spaced cedars dot the lawn beside the garden, with several picnic tables strategically placed to catch sunlight. There is a treehouse quality to the viewing platform that overlooks the picnic area. The trunk of a giant fir thrusts up through the middle of the platform. Water music from the Serpentine's tributaries fills the air here.

There were other plans for Tynehead before it became what it is today. For years eastbound drivers on the Trans-Canada Highway saw a sign proclaiming this as the future home of the Tynehead Zoo, but after 15 years of unsuccessfully seeking funds the society that hoped to build what it called a "zoological garden" gave up, and the sign disappeared in late 1990. For much of the year Tynehead park is rather quiet, but that suits the inhabitants of the open fields and hedgerows just fine. They don't need a zoological garden to make them feel at home. As small a reserve as it might be, Tynehead Park *is* their home.

Over the years since the zoological garden concept was shelved there have been a number of improvements to Tynehead park. The Greater Vancouver Regional District has also decided not to allow any major development on the flood plain of the Serpentine River or its tributaries. The continuing emphasis at Tynehead is to protect the forest canopy of original and introduced species of trees, and to preserve the park for wildlife in the face of increasing pressure from the public. The park's proximity to Surrey's residential neighbourhoods is clearly a mixed blessing, and the ability to preserve wilderness side by side with development will be the major challenge faced by the politicians and GVRD park planners in the years ahead.

18 | SERPENTINE FEN

NATURE OBSERVATION ◄
PICNICKING ◄
WALKING ◄

As you drive south on Highway 99 where it curves around the east end of Mud Bay, you pass underneath the hydro lines that straddle the highway, 1.2 mi. (2 km) before the Crescent Beach/White Rock exit. A tall wooden observation tower stands out on the east side as the highway passes over the Serpentine River. Farther east you can see yet another of these.

To get a better look at the towers, exit Highway 99 at Crescent Beach and head north on the King George Highway for a short distance to 44th Avenue. (An Art Knapp Plantland garden nursery is located at this junction.) Turn left and drive in to the parking lot and picnic area. Several tables are conveniently arranged in a sheltered grove away from the breeze that often blows in off nearby Mud Bay. The main trail begins here, and you can walk it easily in an hour.

The tower isn't hard to find, being the tallest structure on the Serpentine fen, as the open delta at the river's mouth is called (on the evolutionary scale, fens lie between swamps and bogs). Together with its companion tower, the observation tower turns out to be located at the Serpentine Wildlife Management Area. Ducks Unlimited released 260 Canada geese here in 1973, and a series of trails loop around several ponds created with funds from the Sportsmen of Northern California and the B.C. government. The refuge provides sheltered nesting grounds for the fat ducks and geese that winter locally. Judging from the current Canada goose population in the fen, the project was an unqualified success. These days the fen geese compete for air space with ultralight aircraft that fly from a nearby field.

Bird-watching on the fen's Nature Walk trail

The level trail that runs beside the open ponds makes a figure-eight through the fen. It's hard-packed, so that even in wet weather footwear is not a problem. Several bridges cross small channels that provide water for the ponds from the nearby Serpentine River. On sunny days there's not much shade to be found except under the roofs of the two observation towers. In keeping with its design as a wildlife habitat, the fen is a quiet environment with only the background hum of traffic as a reminder of the outside world. When fog rolls in it can be even more splendidly isolated.

With such a welcoming location the Serpentine fen provides a stopover for more than Canada geese. A variety of dabbling and diving ducks—including goldeneyes, mergansers and mallards—spend time here during spring and fall migration times. If you're interested in a guided birding tour of the fen, contact Wings 'N Things Nature Tours, 922-2176.

19 | NICOMEKL RIVER

BOATING ◄
DRIVING ◄
FISHING ◄
PADDLING ◄
PICNICKING ◄
SIGHTSEEING ◄
SWIMMING ◄
WALKING ◄

Two major tributaries flow into Mud Bay: the Serpentine and Nicomekl rivers. Of the two, the Nicomekl is the most accessible for exploration from Mud Bay or a variety of locations inland. Drive around, scouting as you go for the place that best suits your tastes, then boat it, bike it, beach it—it's up to you.

There's lots to enjoy along the banks of the river in the Crescent Beach region, especially around Elgin, an old pioneer community of South Surrey. Winding Crescent Road parallels the Nicomekl and offers several locations of interest to day trippers, including Elgin Heritage Park, Crescent Park, the Canadian Aviation Museum and Blackie Spit and Crescent Beach parks where the Nicomekl meets the Pacific.

Finding your way around this area of South Surrey can be somewhat confusing if you haven't visited here before. Therefore, my recommendation is that you take a few minutes upon arrival in the Crescent Beach neighbourhood to familiarize yourself with the layout of the roads.

ELGIN HERITAGE PARK   To get to Elgin Heritage Park from Vancouver, take the White Rock-Crescent Beach turnoff (Exit 10) from Highway 99. You immediately have two choices: take either the first right onto Elgin Road, or the second right onto King George Highway (Highway 99A). Both connect with Crescent Road. From the Esso station on Elgin, follow Crescent Road as it leads west towards Crescent Beach; or, from King George Highway, join Crescent at the first set of stoplights west of Highway 99. Elgin

Heritage Park is located 1.2 mi. (2 km) west of King George Highway on Crescent Road.

Several signs of the old community of Elgin appear along the way, including the Elgin Community Hall on the south side of the road. The rock cairn next to the nearby Esso station features a plaque outlining the history of the old Elgin Trail. A right turn at the Esso station will put you on Elgin Road, which crosses the Nicomekl on a small bridge above a dam that regulates the outflow into Mud Bay.

At the south end of this one-lane, one-way (southbound only) bridge is a rough area useful for launching hand-carried boats. If you have come from Vancouver on Highway 99 and taken Elgin Road upon exiting, you can park on the north side of the Nicomekl next to the bright green King George Bridge: turn left onto Nicomekl Road, just before the one-lane Elgin Road bridge. (This may sound complicated, but you'll see that it's quite straightforward once you've made your first visit.) You'll find both parking and launching easier from this location.

Elgin Heritage Park is on the site of the Stewart farmhouse, built on the shore of the Nicomekl in 1894 and restored in 1984–85. There is a beautiful pole barn where a variety of machinery is now stored, and an outbuilding on a sheltered part of the property is home to the Sooner Weaving Centre. The lawn in front of the barn, recently planted with a variety of apple trees, makes a pleasant picnic location. An old trail heads east from the barn beside the river, leading off towards the Nico Wynd Golf Club. In summer there is excellent berry-picking next to the path (which is more of an overgrown wagon trail).

PADDLING THE NICOMEKL   Exploration of the Nicomekl, a river that spends a lot of its length winding through Surrey on its search for the ocean, can begin as far west as Crescent Beach, Wards Boat Launch at Elgin Park, the Elgin or King George bridges or several locations farther east, depending on the amount of time at your disposal. Wards Boat Launch is on the river side of the Stewart farmhouse. There is plenty of room for parking here. You can launch from a ramp or from a dock. Note the boathouse's carved door with its weathered native Indian design.

The Nicomekl is wide enough for several canoes to travel in tandem without infringing on the occasional river traffic coming from the opposite direction. One of the joys of exploring it is

Gentle canoeing on the Nicomekl River

the tranquillity of the environment in contrast to the hum of traffic speeding by on the nearby autoroutes. Farther east on the river the surroundings become more agricultural as you enter the Cloverdale Valley. It's rather fun to paddle beneath the series of bridges spanning the river, especially those over which you may have hurried in your car on the way to the border or into Crescent Beach and White Rock. There's no sense of urgency on the Nicomekl. High banks shield most activity outside the realm of the river from sight. With such a limited horizon—just you, the river and the sky above—there's time to indulge in a private daydream or two.

Just east of where Highway 99 carries traffic across the Nicomekl is a hillside covered with tall trees, to the south of the river. Large owls can be spotted roosting here, along with a host of raptors and other birds. Horses graze in the open fields below the ridge. The stretch of river between the Highway 99 bridge and a much smaller span on 40th Avenue is a pleasant length to cover in the course of an afternoon. Large steelhead can occasionally be seen flashing silver just below the surface of the water. Fishing is popular at a variety of locations, including beneath the footings of the 152nd Street bridge. A catch-and-release program is in effect for steelhead here; you are allowed to keep two rainbow trout a day, should you be so lucky.

There is a very rough launching area beside the 40th Avenue bridge with a small pull-off for one vehicle on each side. There is also limited parking beside 40th Avenue. If you have set out from Elgin Road, this may be as far as you wish to venture in one day before heading back.

Northeast of here the river flows through fields planted with blueberries, corn and a variety of other crops. The quiet monotony of the paddle from 40th Avenue east may be a bit too laid-back for some adventurers. For others, though, with no particular destination in mind, the pace on the Nicomekl in these parts will be idyllic. The wind whispering through the tall heads of grass offers wise counsel indeed. Brambles cover the high banks in many places. In late summer the trick will be to find a location where you can pick the blackberries as they mature. But watch out—as you reach to grasp the berries, the vines reach to snare you!

The Nicomekl maintains this serene setting and pace until it reaches 176th Street, several hours' paddle one way from the 40th Avenue bridge east of 152nd Street. There is also a bridge at 168th Street and 48th Avenue, but the banks are too steep to launch here. A better approach is the bridge at 184th Street just north of 44th Avenue.

Cloverdale, one of Surrey's five central hubs, lies just north of the 168th Street bridge. If you're out for a leisurely drive, this is an excellent area in which to buy fresh vegetables and fruit from roadside stands, particularly along 152nd and 168th streets between Highway 10 and 40th Avenue. Also, on the west side of 168th Street between 50th Avenue and Colebrook Road, watch for a most unusual display of hubcaps affixed to the side of a large barn and on two tall poles at the entrance of a farm north of the bridge over the Nicomekl.

There are not many places to picnic along the Nicomekl east

of Elgin Heritage Park, particularly in spring and early summer months when the river is running high, but one or two locations always present themselves as potential landing spots. When you find one, climb to the top of the riverbank for a look around. Invariably wide-open fields will await you, and after your break you can return to the river happily, knowing that all is serene in the outside world. At times during the day the water's surface becomes completely calm, reflecting perfectly the hue of the riverbank, be it the deep green of spring or the burnished gold of late summer, as colourful as a drift of alpine flowers. The stillness of the river makes it a wonderful place to experience a moonrise. At times, there will be a hint of fog and perhaps a crispness in the air around a harvest moon that will set you thinking of pumpkins oranging somewhere nearby.

As you round a corner, a territorially sensitive heron may take flight, croaking its displeasure at you. Hawks, wild canaries, killdeers and plovers will fly overhead while you sit quietly on the shore, though when you first venture onto the river you may wonder where all the birds are hiding. Once you take up a position and they become used to your presence, you'll discover that you have plenty of company as the birds return to the routine that you unknowingly interrupted with your arrival.

Out here the weather can be sunnier than in Vancouver. There seems to be a dividing line where clouds thin out above south Surrey, leaving the darker ones to bump up against the North Shore mountains. This is not to say that Surrey doesn't get its share of moisture, as is evident at bridges and bends in the river where matted, mud-caked debris has been deposited in branches and cross-spars at times of high water. When the Nicomekl is cresting is the best time to put in at one of the bridges, such as at 184th Street north of 44th Avenue, and let the current carry you downstream. Perhaps you can organize two vehicles, one to be left where you launch and the other at a prearranged pull-out location, allowing you to make a lengthy one-way trip on the Nicomekl.

LANGLEY   East of 184th Street the Nicomekl narrows as it nears the border of Surrey and Langley. By the time it reaches 196th Street the streambed has shrunk to a narrow 16 ft. (5 m). West of 192nd Street at High Knoll Park on Colebrook Road (50th Avenue) you can walk out into the meadow, where a trail leads from the parking lot to a wooden pedestrian bridge across the Nicomekl. The wooded park has a web of trails suitable for walking or cycling.

Once in Langley, housing development begins to crowd in on each side of the Nicomekl. By the time it crosses 200th Street between 50th and 53rd avenues the Nicomekl has established a reputation for itself as a flood-plain river and it's carefully controlled east of here to its source at 240th Street near Robertson Crescent. The Nicomekl Flood Plain Park in Langley begins at 200th Street. A rough path follows the river as it winds towards its confluence with Murray Creek at the Langley Bypass.

The municipalities through which the Nicomekl flows take great interest in seeing that the river is kept free of debris. For this reason it's possible to explore the river from source to sea without encountering many obstacles along most of its length. As more of us frequent the Nicomekl in small boats or walk its banks in search of that prized fishing hole, we should all do what we can to keep it pristine.

20 | REDWOOD PARK

PICNICKING ◄
TOBOGGANING ◄
VIEWPOINTS ◄
WALKING ◄

Redwood Park in South Surrey's Hazelmere Valley is a quiet little afternoon getaway. Trails run through the shaded forest on a bluff overlooking farmland on both sides of the border, and there are picnic tables and a children's playground next to the parking lot.

To find Redwood Park, go south on the King George Highway to 20th Avenue, east to 180th Street, then south two blocks to the park entrance. Alternatively, from Highway 99 drive east on 16th Avenue to 177th Street. Watch for the trailhead leading into Redwood Park on the north side of 16th Avenue just east of 177th Street.

Surrey is B.C.'s newest city, and the second largest in the province. Its incorporation as a municipality in 1879 predated Vancouver's by seven years, but development was slow on the peat marshes and glacial till where early residents made their homes. Many of the original settlers came from the Prairies during the Great Depression, and they worked the soil and cut the forests. In the 1930s the community was faced with the decision of whether or not to log the last stand of original timber in Surrey: alas, they did. Not everyone in Surrey supported the destruction of the forest, and at this South Surrey park a tall stand of redwoods has been planted and protected.

Redwood Park was the home of two brothers, David and Peter Brown, who arrived in South Surrey in the late 1870s. They bought farmland in the Hazelmere Valley in 1893 and lived there until 1958. Trees were as much a part of their lives as the open fields that ran along the ridge of their property on the North

Gnarled winter trees in Redwood Park

Bluff Road. The brothers planted 32 species of trees native to Europe, Asia and North America. The most successful of all, the tall redwoods bordering the fields, tower above the rest.

The Browns' redwoods have found a home from which they can look south towards distant Humboldt County in northern California, where their cousins attain greater heights than any other tree species in the world. Four adult humans holding hands can just encircle the biggest redwood in the park. And these are only young trees—imagine how much bigger they'll be this time next century!

Carved on a sheltered sign at the beginning of the trail through Redwood Park is the Prayer of the Woods, setting a tone for the rest of your visit:

> I am the heat of your hearth on the cold winter nights, the friendly shade screening you from the summer sun, and my fruits are refreshing draughts quenching your thirst as you journey. I am the beam that holds your house, the board of your table, the bed on which you lie, and the timber that builds your boat. I am the handle of your hoe, the door of your homestead, the wood of your cradle, and the shell of your coffin. I am the bread of kindness and the flower of beauty. Ye who pass by, listen to my prayer. Harm me not.

Over the years the Browns had several different homes on the property, each of which was destroyed by fire. Finally they built a tree house in the middle of the forest. This one lasted. A long ramp led up to the door of their home, which was sturdily perched a storey above the forest floor. The original was taken down in 1986, but a replica has been installed in its place and is available for use by groups. Call the Fairfax recreation office to get the key (591-4426).

Other tall evergreens add to the park's mosaic. From November through March, when most of the deciduous trees have shed their leaves and the gnarled branches dance and sway like many-armed Shivas in the wind, Redwood Park is a pleasant stop on a cold day, sheltering visitors from wind and rain. After a snowfall, the open ridges beside the forest will be thrilling to ride on a toboggan. Sheltered barbecues and a secluded campfire area—an unusual feature in a suburban park—are among the other attractions here.

21 | MUD BAY

CYCLING ◄
NATURE OBSERVATION ◄
PICNICKING ◄
VIEWPOINTS ◄
WALKING ◄

Mud Bay: where the hulls of ships come home to bottom out. Where light aircraft practise touch-and-go manoeuvres while flocks of sandpipers fly evasion formations at the tideline. Where an ancient cannery stands shaking and stranded on creosoted pylons. Where Anne's Koffeeport in the Delta Air Park has a booth waiting for you.

Mud Bay is the junior member of a triad of bays, a broad, shallow expanse of gumbo on the border where Delta and South Surrey meet. Boundary and Semiahmoo bays are its senior partners. You pass beside Mud Bay each time you drive along Highway 99 between Ladner and Crescent Beach. Only the Burlington Northern railway line gets to cross the waters: the rest of us road travellers have to circle around it.

Much of the time Mud Bay looks as if someone has pulled the plug and forgotten to clean the tub. Two rivers, the Serpentine and Nicomekl, empty into the bay's eastern end. They bring silt from headwaters many miles inland. This is the source of all that mud, deposited year after year by run-off.

Beginning earlier in this century, crude dikes were built around the shorelines of Mud and Boundary bays to hold back the ocean. They have been improved considerably in the years since then. Truck gardeners and turf farmers are still the main occupants of the land in behind the dikes. A few cows, sheep and horses are pastured around the old Delta homesteads that lie sprinkled along the roads leading down to the bays. Urban sprawl is eating up many of the fields closer to Tsawwassen, but down around Mud Bay agricultural reserve land still holds sway.

Old cannery on Mud Bay

When hard-packed, dike trails are wonderfully level surfaces to roll along on a bicycle, and the one on the north side of Mud Bay is no exception. As you pass the bay on Highway 99 you can see signs of a trail in the distance, but access to the dike from the main highway is limited. If you take the Highway 10 exit off 99 you'll be within a mile of the bay. The only other alternative is to take the Highway 17 exit and get onto the Ladner Trunk Road (Highway 10 under another name) heading east.

If you take the Highway 10 exit, cross south onto Hornby Drive at the first set of stoplights. There is an RCMP detachment at this intersection. Take the first right turn off Hornby onto 96th Street and drive to the south end. There is parking on the dike and beside the road (on road maps of the area the dike is referred to as Irwin Road). A gate bars vehicle access east of here, and you can drive only a short distance west on Irwin Road before it dead-ends. At this point you're no longer on Mud Bay, having come out onto much larger Boundary Bay. As if to make the distinction clear, beyond is the Boundary Bay airport, much grander in turn than the nearer Delta Air Park.

Another approach is to stay on Hornby to 104th Street, following the signs to the Delta Air Park. You may find that parking is limited here, especially on busy weekends. Nonetheless, if you are travelling with small children this might be the better approach as it's closer to the heart of Mud Bay.

The surface of the dike is wide enough for walkers, bikers and horseriders to share. Hawks, eagles and owls patrol the fields on one side, while on the other shorebirds in the thousands flock back and forth. The sandpipers are particularly active. Their ability to instantly change direction in midflight is a survival technique against raptors. To onlookers they present an ever-changing pattern in white and black: one moment they are a white cloud, the next they blend invisibly with the dark background of the ocean.

As you progress along the dike eastward from 96th Street you pass the small airport out of which the Boundary Bay Flying Club operates. Several dozen light planes of various vintages are parked here. If the wind is blowing cool off the bay you may wish to visit the small café next to the runway for a quick warmup. Anne's Koffeeport is the kind of place you wish there were more of around the countryside in the Lower Mainland. It's clean and friendly, with pictures of airplanes covering the walls.

Mud Bay comes into its own east of the air park. The dike leads towards an old cannery at the foot of 112th Street, perhaps the last of its kind in the Fraser delta. Judging from its dilapidation, it must have ceased operations in the 1950s, but no one has torn it down, yet. It's possessed of a crazed appearance, reminiscent of Van Gogh's painting of his room at Arles.

The surface of the dike becomes increasingly rough as you proceed east from here. A point of land jutting out into the water forces the dike to curve inland for a short while before parallelling the bay once more. Here and there are shells of old boats, mired in the mud. Highway 99 edges closer to the trail until only a small fence separates the two. The surface of the dike is loose gravel or sand, and the going is tough if you're wheeling a bike or a stroller. The trail swings away from the highway after 10 minutes of this. Your reward will be some isolated viewing sites on the bay's shoreline, perfect picnic spots.

The trail dead-ends where it meets up with the Burlington Northern railway line. A long wooden bridge carries the track across Mud Bay. The dike continues on the other side of the tracks but access is restricted by a barbed wire fence. If you've come by bike it will take an hour of steady riding to return from here to 96th Street.

Before you go, find a seat on the driftwood "furniture" here and take time to admire the light show over the bay. The mud is speckled with small ponds of water that reflect the colour of the sky; sunlight striking the surface of the ponds turns them a silvery blue colour. One of my favourite times of the day for making this journey is in late afternoon, when the bay lights up with a unique brilliance all its own.

22 | PEACE ARCH PROVINCIAL PARK

CYCLING ◄
DRIVING ◄
PADDLING ◄
PICNICKING ◄
SIGHTSEEING ◄
VIEWPOINTS ◄
WALKING ◄
◄

Usually when we pass through Peace Arch park we're on our way to somewhere else. It may seem like a strange concept to head for the Canada-U.S. border without actually intending to go any farther. When confronted by a lineup of vehicles waiting to clear customs—up to an hour's worth on certain days, except for those with a Peace Arch Crossing Experiment (PACE) sticker—some passengers have probably gotten out of the car, perhaps with the family pet, for a quick stroll past the extensive flower beds. Perhaps, while inching along in the car, you've wondered about the groups enjoying a picnic barbecue at the beautifully maintained shelter on the Canadian side, or having their pictures taken in front of the gazebo beside the lily pond. (When you visit the gazebo, be sure to look up at the interior ceiling. The sectioned roof is constructed of wood from eight different B.C. native trees, beautifully lacquered. It's interesting to compare the patterns made by the various grains.)

Scattered about the park are 41 picnic tables. The large picnic shelter, open to all, is available for groups of 20 or more and has a kitchen equipped with hotplates and sinks. Outside the shelter is a children's adventure playground. There is another playground on the American side next to 0 Avenue.

Once you begin to explore Peace Arch park you'll understand why it's a favourite site for wedding parties for photos on a sunny afternoon. The lovingly tended flower beds provide a colourful backdrop. And there's a certain giddy feeling to walking back and forth across the border—officially, a strip 40 ft. (12 m) wide, originally cleared in 1857—that's difficult to describe.

Perhaps it's the ease with which you can wander between the two countries on foot, compared to the waiting and fretting of coping with border officials when crossing by car.

While the ambience of Peace Arch park is a major part of its attraction, especially during months when the flowers are in peak bloom and a cooling breeze wafts in from Semiahmoo Bay, the centrepiece, the Peace Arch itself, is impossible to ignore. Tourists from outside North America have a special fascination with the monument when it comes to taking pictures. Yet many passers-by who have made Vancouver their home may not fathom the true worth and significance of the imposing white monument, the only symbol of its kind erected at any border crossing in the world.

You can acquaint yourself with the arch's history through a series of informative displays mounted throughout the park on both sides of the border. (British Columbia maintains 22 acres/ 9 ha of park north of the 49th parallel, while Washington State takes responsibility for 17 acres/7 ha on the southern side.) The original initiative to build a monument commemorating the lasting peace that exists between Canada and the United States came from Samuel Hill, an American road and railway builder from Seattle. As a member of the Quaker Church, Hill sought to promote global peace in all of his undertakings. Among other accomplishments, he was the president of the Pacific Highway Association and responsible for the development of the first transportation links on the west coast between Washington State and British Columbia.

Hill conceived the idea for a peace monument on July 4, 1915, as the First World War was gathering momentum in Europe. The original arch was a wooden affair constructed over the railway line that skirts Semiahmoo Bay. At the time there was no road leading from Vancouver to the border; it would be many years before one was built. In its own way, the magnetism of the Peace Arch attracted support for construction of a road.

The Peace Arch as we know it now was dedicated on September 6, 1921. Both Samuel Hill and Mayor Wells Gray of New Westminster were present. (Although there is a creek named for Sam Hill located in nearby South Surrey, there does not appear to have been any reciprocal gesture to Wells Gray in Whatcom County.) Built of concrete reinforced with steel, the Peace Arch is designed to vibrate but not crack during an earthquake. In

The Peace Arch

1993, the arch was given an extensive upgrading. A number of plaques affixed to the sides of the monument reveal various historical connections. One bears a likeness of the steamship *Beaver*. The original wooden Peace Arch contained a piece of wood from two English vessels of renown: the *Beaver*, in 1836 the first steamship to sail the Pacific from Europe, and the *Mayflower*, the ship that brought members of the Pilgrim brethren to America in 1620.

One important fact about the creation of Peace Arch Park should not be allowed to escape mention: donations from schoolchildren on both sides of the border were primarily responsible for raising the funds required to purchase land for the park. Each year on the second Sunday in June, thousands of children and adults gather in the park for a Hands Across the Border celebration.

If you are making the park your ultimate destination rather than passing through on your way south of the border, the easiest approach is to take Highway 99 almost to the Canada Customs and Immigration Building, then turn off onto Beach Road, next to the duty-free store. Watch for a sign pointing the way to Peace Arch Provincial Park. Follow Beach Road a short distance towards Semiahmoo Bay, then turn left off Beach to reach the park entrance.

(Beach Road runs north beside Semiahmoo Bay and its confluence with the Campbell River, through the Semiahmoo Indian Reserve. There is a boat launch from where you can explore the Campbell River estuary, a site rich in wildlife, sequestered behind the sheltering banks that support the Burlington Northern Railroad tracks. A wooden pedestrian bridge crosses over Campbell River to Semiahmoo Park and the White Rock seawall from the reserve. Tie this in to a visit to Peace Arch park and you'll have a full day's worth of exploration on your hands. Note: there is no access to the beach on Semiahmoo Bay from Peace Arch park.)

Use the parking lot at Peace Arch park as your staging area for whatever else you've planned. Large picnic shelters are located in both the Canadian and American sides of the park. The one on the Canadian side is most visible; the American shelter is concealed behind the flower beds on the hill to the east of the Peace Arch and Highway 99.

23 | IONA BEACH REGIONAL PARK

BIRD-WATCHING ◄
CYCLING ◄
DRIVING ◄
PADDLING ◄
PICNICKING ◄
STARGAZING ◄
VIEWPOINTS ◄
WALKING ◄

Iona Island is a wild, windswept place, with a slender scissor-shaped nose jutting out into Sturgeon Bank, ending at Point No Point. Only a short drive or bike ride from downtown Vancouver, it sits at the mouth of the north arm of the Fraser River, with the Musqueam Indian Reserve across the water on one hand, and Sea Island (site of the international airport) on the other. The park here has had a major facilities upgrade since it was taken over by the Greater Vancouver Regional District in 1990, including a new interpretive centre between the parking lot and the beach. From there you can fan out to explore the sheltered or exposed sides of the island so evidently shaped by sediment dumped at the ocean's doorstep by the mighty Fraser River.

To find your way to Iona Island, take the Arthur Laing Bridge at the south end of Granville Street, following the Richmond exit to the right as soon as you reach the south end of the bridge. Bear left to follow the off-ramp towards Miller Road, staying in the left-hand lane as you approach the stop sign. From there, a green GVRD sign points left to Iona Park. Follow the signs from here as Miller runs into Grauer, then McDonald, and finally Ferguson Road on the west side of Sea Island.

As you travel across Sea Island it's impossible to ignore the airport, especially now that construction of the third runway is under way. You'll see signs directing you towards Iona, as well as McDonald Beach and Woods Island Park, a Richmond municipal park.

(A boat-launch ramp leads down to a small indentation off

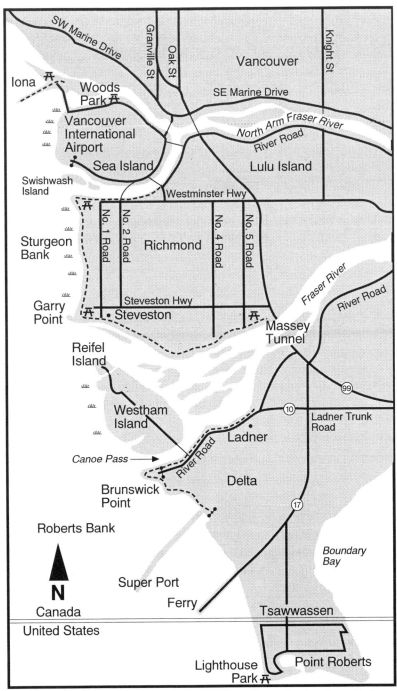

Fraser Estuary: Iona Island to Point Roberts

the Fraser at McDonald Beach. You can put in here and paddle west to explore Iona Island. Picnic tables are spread out atop the dike. A concession and bait stand is also open here most days.)

As you near the park entrance the road passes over a causeway built in the early part of this century to link Sea Island and Iona. McDonald Slough, on the east side of the road, is often choked with log booms. The road swings west past the sewage treatment plant to the park gates. Leave your car here if you plan on being in the park after sunset, as the gate is locked at dusk except on special occasions, such as stargazing evenings.

During the day birders fill their eyes with the sights of Iona's migrating flocks; stargazing visitors benefit from the increased darkness of the sky here, unhindered by the glare of city streetlights. The GVRD's free Catch a Falling Star astronomy program brings high-powered telescopes from the Southam Observatory to Iona on a regular basis. There are also slide shows at the interpretive centre and hot refreshments available to ward off the crisp night air. On all your trips to Iona, be sure to dress warmly, including a hat to protect your ears against the wind blowing off the Strait of Georgia. For the stargazing program, bring your own chair, mug and those ever-trusty binoculars.

Iona Island is a stopover for thousands of migrating birds. According to marine biologist Peggy Ward, more rare birds are seen here than anywhere else in the province. Mallards and teals dabble in the ocean over the tidal flats. Loons, grebes and herons fill their long curved gullets with abundant marine life found in the sheltered lagoons. Pairs of round-faced great horned, short-eared and screech owls glide by on silent wings; rare burrowing owls occasionally nest in the sand dunes that cover much of the island. Binoculars will help you see right into the thick of the flocks of dunlin that gather by the thousands on the shoreline. Depending on the height of the tide, they can be as close as the parking lot when you arrive, or you may have to head out along the long southern jetty to see them feed while the ocean ebbs. When startled, they lift off in a dizzying pattern of alternating black and white as they swoop and swirl. A predator would be hard-pressed to tell where the flock is from one moment to the next.

But you don't need binoculars to see bird life at close range. Stalk the gently rolling reaches of the island. Find a sheltered spot beside a lagoon and watch as it comes to life, revealing

128

Looking north from Iona to UBC

itself as you wait in patient stillness. A quiet season like autumn lends itself to such unobtrusive observation.

When the Greater Vancouver Regional District assumed control over Iona, one of its first steps was to instal a gate on the approach road. Dune buggies and dirt bikes no longer power their way around the island, and calm has returned to the former farmland (Iona was originally homesteaded in 1885). As well, the island's air quality is no longer as strongly influenced by the nearby sewage treatment plant, thanks to a new outfall pipe, and the 2.5-mi. (4-km) jetty over which the pipeline runs is now a hard-packed gravel walkway. There are two plexiglass shelters, located at the middle and end of the jetty, that allow visitors to escape the winds that blow across the Strait of Georgia, and at the same time provide an unobstructed bird's-eye view of Sturgeon Bank. Across the strait, Vancouver Island is outlined against the western sky. Closer, the mountains on the North Shore stand out, with no office towers blocking the view. For photographers who enjoy capturing a sunrise or sunset, these shelters are ideal places to position a camera.

Throughout the year the GVRD offers a variety of interpretive programs at Iona for all ages. One of my favourites is the Marsh Planting Bee, in which visitors are given the chance to transplant bulrushes, sedges, cattails and reeds into the shallow waters of the park. Efforts like these will pay dividends in the coming years as the plants provide a ready source of food and nesting habitat for birds and also help restore the marsh. Park officials hope to attract more yellow-headed blackbirds, extremely rare on the Lower Mainland, to make their home on Iona's restored marshland.

Another program invites young children to participate in a Dune Sifters adventure walk. Led by a park interpreter, kids investigate the shifting dunes, follow bird-calls and discover unusual forms of intertidal life. While children are being entertained, parents have the chance to do some exploring of their own.

Bring your bikes with you, as the causeway at Iona is level, and there's easy riding through the nearby farmland on Sea Island. River traffic on the Fraser and aircraft landing and taking off at Vancouver International Airport contribute to the scene.

Other seasonal events at Iona are held in the early morning or early evening hours to introduce visitors of all ages to birding. Basic bird identification, using habitat, colour, behaviour and song clues, is taught over a two-hour period. There is a modest charge for these courses; visitors should register in advance by calling the GVRD at 432-6351. Also ask for a complete outline of the programs scheduled for the months ahead.

24 LULU ISLAND
DIKE TRAILS

BIRD-WATCHING ◄
CYCLING ◄
DRIVING ◄
PADDLING ◄
PICNICKING ◄
SIGHTSEEING ◄
SWIMMING ◄
VIEWPOINTS ◄
WALKING ◄

Lulu Island is held in the embrace of all three arms of the Fraser River, with seven bridges and the Massey Tunnel connecting it to the rest of the Lower Mainland. The island is ringed by 48 mi. (77 km) of dikes, much of which is useful as walking or riding trails. Because there's more here than most of us can cover in a day, Lulu Island always leaves us eager to return for further explorations.

Sea Island (home of the Vancouver International Airport) and most of Lulu Island, as well as a number of smaller islands in the Fraser, comprise the municipality of Richmond. So why isn't this called Richmond Island? In this case, blame Colonel Moody of the Royal Engineers, who had been surveying much of the Fraser estuary in 1862: he named this tract of unsettled land, the largest island at the mouth of the river, after visiting actress Miss Lulu Sweet. There are certain things that can only happen in a frontier setting . . .

At almost the same time the McRoberts family, which had recently emigrated from Australia to Sea Island, named their new property Richmond Farms after one daughter's favourite place in their last home. These two names, Lulu and Richmond, have vied for dominance from the beginning.

There's a special spot on Lulu Island that has drawn settlers since the turn of the century—former citizens of Finland, Japan and the sovereign nation of Newfoundland, for instance. The first arrivals gathered on the southwestern corner of the island at Steveston, named for a member of the Steves family, which settled here in 1877 upon their arrival from New Brunswick. By

1889 the oldest son, William Herbert Steves, had begun dividing the property into town lots, and the Steveston real estate boom was under way.

Construction of protective dikes along the western shore of Lulu Island was one of the first priorities for the newcomers. These have been improved with time and now provide a level surface that stretches for miles. Many of the old farm homes have disappeared, but enough of the original flavour remains to make this westerly stretch of dike and historic Steveston a must-see for local adventurers.

It's also a jumping-off point for exploring the whole of Richmond's western shore. Take an hour or plan an entire day to enjoy the surroundings. As long as you aren't travelling at peak traffic periods, the 17-mi. (27-km) drive from downtown Vancouver to the dike and Steveston docks takes all of 20 minutes on Highway 99 South. Take the Steveston Highway West exit. You'll pass Fantasy Gardens, the Vancouver Buddhist Church with its two dragons of good fortune atop the ornate roof, and a series of fruit and vegetable stands where locally grown produce is available at bargain prices.

STEVESTON VILLAGE   A narrow road runs behind the private wharves that lead from Garry Point to the Steveston public dock. The Gulf of Georgia Cannery Interpretive Centre is on Fourth Avenue directly behind Canfisco. It's operated by Parks Canada and contains relics from the past, when the canneries operated night and day. (At one time, 49 canneries were in operation at Steveston.) A model production line is set up along one long L-shaped counter, with small figurines representing the employees dressed in outfits from the 1930s. Murals of fish and trawlers cover the walls: showcases full of glass fishing balls from Japan, shiny salmon tins and model boats all help convey a sense of Steveston's heritage. There are mountains of fishing gear and nets arranged outside. The interpretive centre is open Wednesday to Sunday between 10 A.M. and 5 P.M.

A directory to historic Steveston is posted at the corner of Third Avenue and Moncton Street, one block from the government wharf and kitty-corner to the Steveston Hotel (with its unique drive-through liquor off-sales window in back). Cafés, gift shops and a thriving bike shop located in an old church building all add to the local charm. The Japanese influence on the village is still evident in new developments like the Okana Court on First Avenue between Chatham and Moncton, where the Nikaido gift shop features kimonos.

The focal point of Steveston's redevelopment is the public wharf. Fishing boats with poetic names are tied up along rows of docks. You can buy seafood directly from many of the boats, and shrimp, squid, snapper, tuna, sole, cod and salmon are all available—in season—at good prices. For those with an immediate hunger, a floating café and a restaurant nearby on the dock serve up fish and chips along with a local favourite, steaming mushy peas. Several new buildings constructed nearby retain the architectural flavour of old Steveston.

If you wish to explore Steveston and the west dikes by bike, rentals can be arranged at Steveston Bikes, at Second Avenue and Chatham (271-5544). They also rent trailers to tow behind. Oh, to be a kid again and see Steveston from a trailer!

GARRY POINT PARK   If you drive to the western end of Steveston Highway, where it meets the dike at Seventh Avenue, you'll find parking for six vehicles. In another two minutes you can be at Garry Point Park, with parking for 60. Simply drive several blocks south along Seventh to reach the park. It's located two blocks west of the federal wharf, which forms the heart of revitalized Steveston. There's more parking available on the shoulders of Chatham and neighbouring streets.

Early on weekend mornings, groups of kayakers assemble at Garry Point while families on bikes head north along the dike trail and sunlovers perch on the driftwood of nearby beaches. The Canadian Coast Guard hydrofoil skims noisily past, throwing up seaspray around its rubber skirts as it patrols the mouth of the Fraser River and around into Cannery Channel. Long-necked Steveston Island, shaped like a crane's profile, lies directly offshore, shielding parts of the river and the town of Ladner on the far shore from view. A small Japanese rock garden, opened in 1988, draws the attention of grandparents and toddlers alike; it is dedicated to the memory of the first immigrants from Japan's Wakayama Prefecture, who arrived in 1888.

For those with rubber boots and a desire to get out onto nearby Sturgeon Bank, a humpty-dumpty trail heads off the main trail at Garry Point and out into the marsh just north of a weathered marina's dock and boathouse. The brackish marsh renews its vegetation of cattails, bulrushes, eelgrass and sedges every spring, and the air here is filled with bird calls. You can often count a half-dozen or more different territorial melodies at once, punctuated by the incongruous crowing of a rooster from a nearby farm. Although there are picnic tables at several spots along the dike trail, out on Sturgeon Bank you'll have to make do with a piece of driftwood. You can see here what much of Lulu Island must have looked like before dikes began to reclaim the land in the first half of this century.

The dike runs in an almost-straight north-south line along the western perimeter of Lulu Island, a distance of 3.4 mi. (5.5 km). It's well used, especially on weekends. You can ride along the level trail at an easy pace, covering the entire distance one way in approximately 40 minutes. The busiest section of the trail is around the Quilchena Golf Course; north of this the dike can be quite deserted at times. A drainage channel runs parallel to the dike along its eastern side. Small private bridges link the dike with many of the back yards across the ditch. There are numerous fine examples of intensive gardening here; one homeowner has taken the "sunken bath" concept to new heights (or is that depths?) by installing no fewer than six old tubs in his garden for use as planters, filling them with rich alluvial soil from the delta.

MIDDLE ARM DIKE TRAIL As the dike trail rounds the northwestern tip of Lulu Island it passes a parking area at the west end of River Road. There are picnic tables and toilets located here. The Middle Arm of the Fraser River meets the Strait of Georgia at this point. Low-lying Swishwash Island nestles offshore, with Sea Island and the airport beyond to the north. Cold Comfort Farm lies at your back to the south.

In spring months the pungent green smell of willow buds and broom fills the air here. Nearby in the shallows of the Fraser, dabbling ducks, Canada geese, herons and seagulls feast on vegetation and small marine creatures.

The dike trail now runs east along the Middle Arm, past the No. 2 Road, Dinsmore and Moray bridges. The No. 2 Road Bridge, with its circular pedestrian ramp, is the best connection to take you across to Sea Island. A dike trail continues along the banks of the Fraser on Sea Island in both directions. If you

Watching float planes on Moray Channel

head west you pass the south airport and several float-plane wharves and finally arrive at the gates of the Coast Guard station, a comfortable 15-minute ride from the bridge. Nearby is a clearing beside a stand of cottonwoods where you can picnic and watch seaplanes buzz in and out on Moray Channel while jumbo jets arrive and depart. Blackberries are limited but sweet on the brambles overhanging the riverbank. Drifts of wildflowers bloom in summer as purple loosestrife competes with bulrushes for space. (As pretty as the purple loosestrife's tall flower stalks are, this overly successful interloper is having a devastating impact on wildlife habitat throughout the Fraser estuary.) The Fraser estuary is the single most important stopover for millions of birds travelling along the Pacific flyway, such as snow geese (20,000 winter on nearby Westham and Reifel islands), bald eagles, shorebirds and raptors. Sea lions and seals gather offshore in spring for the annual eulachon run. After spawning, these small sardine-sized fish also fall prey to sturgeon, which can reach weights of over half a tonne.

STEVESTON TO WOODWARDS LANDING   One dike trail leads east of Steveston beside the south arm of the Fraser River and runs all the way to the Massey Tunnel. You can cycle this comfortably in half an hour, ending at a small municipal park at the south end of No. 5 Road in an area called Woodwards Landing. As you leave the wharves of Steveston behind you'll pass Gilbert Beach, where a recently built observation platform overlooks the river. Fishing is good here. A broad trail parallels Dyke Road, in back of which is historic London Farm, built just before the turn of the century. Mail and freight once arrived here from Victoria.

Farther east the trail leads past a sleepy backwater known informally as Finn Slough. Ancient boathouses, riverbank shanties and float homes shelter in the lee of Gilmour Island, protected from storms and the wakes of large ocean freighters making their way to or from loading docks farther upriver. If you have a small hand-carried boat you can put in from the riverbank at road's end and explore the slough and Gilmour Island. Just be careful not to become entangled in the blackberry brambles that line much of the shore. If you wish, you can drive directly to Finn Slough at the south end of No. 4 Road. When the tide is out this can be an excellent location to observe shorebirds.

This is also a good spot to pick blackberries, which are usually ripe in August. Blackberry bushes have intimidating thorns, and they lash out at the unsuspecting. Most casual pickers will take only the berries that are most easily reached, leaving the greatest percentage of fruit to those who come prepared. One trick I've learned from watching blackberry harvesters is to bring along some equipment in addition to berry pails. Thick gloves are handy, as is a long hooked pole with which to collar some of the trailing branches that are often laden with fruit but lie tantalizingly beyond reach.

25 | EASTERN LULU AND ANNACIS ISLANDS

BOATING ◄
CYCLING ◄
FISHING ◄
PADDLING ◄
PICNICKING ◄
WALKING ◄

The Fraser River's biggest divide occurs as it meets a delta of islands just downstream from the New Westminster docks. Lulu and Annacis islands are the largest two. At this junction Lulu Island is still part of New Westminster and underpopulated in comparison to its western side, which is home to the municipality of Richmond.

Finding your way to the quiet eastern shores of Lulu and Annacis islands is easy. From Vancouver, take Marine Way east to the Queensborough Bridge. Cross it heading south and take the Boyd Street exit onto Lulu Island. Drive east on Boyd and turn south as it merges with Derwent Way. Drive across the swing bridge over Annacis Channel that leads onto Annacis Island and leave your car in Fraser Port Park. Head back across the bridge to Lulu, where you can begin your explorations on foot or bicycle.

On Lulu's east end you'll discover a small community of river folk still perched on the banks of the channel that separates Lulu and Annacis. There are similarities here to Steveston and Finn Slough at the other end of Lulu Island. Many of the log float homes, cabins and wharves have been standing here for most of the century.

From the looks of things, developers are intent on remaking the face of the area to resemble an unbroken string of pastel-coloured dream homes; however, for the tiniest moment, embers of the old heritage flavour of Lulu Island still flicker on. You can easily fill an afternoon pedalling the length of Dyke Road, peering through the brambles at old boats pulled up in dry dock,

Looking east to New Westminster from Annacis Island

walking out on the occasional public pier to watch traffic on the river or looking across the roofs of float homes to the banks of Annacis Island.

Next to the swing bridge on the Annacis side is small Fraser Port Park, with its sandy-shored fishing bar. Fraser Port Park is one of three riverside parks run by the Fraser Port Authority (the other two are at the north ends of Old Yale and Tannery roads in Surrey, on the south shore of the Fraser River). A large sign at the entrance to Annacis Island welcomes visitors to the district of Delta. Even more of the old flavour of Lulu Island is revealed from Annacis Island; the view across the narrow channel of the old homes and vintage boats, such as *Le Mars* and *La Belle*, is unobstructed.

On a typical Sunday, when the only land traffic on Annacis Island is fellow cyclists, the calm enveloping the river can suddenly be pierced by the wail of a siren. This announcement, like a soulful note from the trumpet of the archangel Gabriel, signals the imminent closing of the swing bridge to motorists. Within minutes the bridge will part to allow a river barge or a tour boat passage through Annacis Channel.

On the east end of Annacis Island, directly across the road from the park and still alongside the channel, are acres of brand-new automobiles. Freshly disembarked from large ocean-going ships that make semiannual visits to ports along the west coast, disgorging vehicles as they go, the shiny new cars and trucks stand in long lines waiting to be loaded onto freight cars for their railway journey to dealerships in the hinterland. As you ride beside them along Annacis Parkway they look like an extra-wide rush-hour gridlock on any major autoroute. The bonus for passing cyclists is that at this point the vehicles aren't putting out any fumes, yet.

On days like this a newly arrived visitor to Lulu and Annacis islands can, as author Kenneth Grahame did when setting the scene for Mole in his classic tale *The Wind in the Willows*, "enter into the joy of running water; and with his ear to the reed stems [catch], at intervals, something of what the wind went whispering so constantly among them."

26 | LADNER DIKE TRAIL

BOATING ◄
CYCLING ◄
PADDLING ◄
PICNICKING ◄
VIEWPOINTS ◄
WALKING ◄

Whether you're exploring the Fraser estuary by car, foot or bicycle, the views are tremendous: the broad expanse of the Strait of Georgia opens on the west; to the north the peaks of the Coast Mountains march along from West Vancouver to Maple Ridge. It's often sunnier out here, too, though cool winds do blow in off the open water. In exposed areas there's little shelter from the wind except behind an accommodating piece of driftwood on the beach. Wherever you wander the ground is level; what's lacking in vertical challenge is made up for in distance.

There are numerous lengthy routes that all bear the common name "River Road" spread throughout the Richmond, Surrey and Delta region. Sometimes River Road runs parallel to a dike trail, while elsewhere the two blend into one.

A particular stretch of dike trail that I enjoy begins in Ladner, an agricultural community first settled by the Ladner brothers in 1868 after they'd had their fling in the Cariboo gold fields. William and Thomas married Mary and Edney, the Booth sisters, and started populating the new settlement, along with former Hudson's Bay Company officers and Colonial Office employees who'd used their discharge pay to purchase prized property at the fertile mouth of the Fraser River. By 1879, Ladner had grown large enough to qualify for municipal status. Along with agriculture, the salmon canneries were the major employers. By 1899, there were 16 canneries in operation in Delta.

Together with nearby Tsawwassen, Ladner grew into the commercial heart of rural Delta. Until the completion of the

140

Massey Tunnel in 1957, residents lived in splendid isolation from Vancouver, a ferry ride to Richmond or the long drive through New Westminster providing the only links. Even today, in the far western reaches of Delta, the ocean breeze sings a haunting song over this secluded area.

To reach Ladner, drive to the south end of the Massey Tunnel and take the first exit right onto River Road. If you miss it, take the next exit right onto Highway 17 South, then turn right again onto Ladner Trunk Road (48th Avenue) for the drive into town.

By taking the River Road exit you approach Ladner on a back road rather than through the community's newer neighbourhoods on Ladner Trunk. One home in particular has been lovingly restored. Watch for it on the south side of River Road soon after you make your exit from Highway 99.

(There are two intersections of note as you travel west on River Road. Turning right on Ferry Road takes you out to the marina on the south side of Deas Slough, glimpsed as you cross the slough on Highway 99. There is a private boat launch here. A right turn at the next road west of Ferry puts you on a paved road that becomes a dirt track, leading around the east end of Ladner Harbour and then west out towards Ladner Harbour Park, a sandy point overlooking Ladner Reach. There is a private marina at road's end.)

As River Road enters downtown Ladner it blends left onto Elliott and then right onto 47A Avenue at the town's major intersection. There are lovely examples of Delta heritage homes to admire as you drive west on 47A, which soon becomes River Road West. (If you're in no hurry, take some time to see Ladner's waterfront by turning left off River Road at Elliott as you enter town. It's only a block long and you can then zigzag your way west through three blocks of back streets, with more heritage homes, to the intersections of 48A Avenue and 48A Street.)

Just west of downtown Ladner the south arm of the Fraser River meets the Strait of Georgia at Roberts Bank, the end of its 850-mi. (1370-km) journey. A large dike protects the town from periodic inundation from ocean tides and river run-off. As the Fraser sweeps past Ladner it curves around Gunn, Barber and Westham islands on the town's north side. Westham is the only one of the three that has been settled. The best place to view these islands is from the top of the dike.

Canoe Passage separates Ladner from diminutive Westham

Dike trail on Brunswick Point

Island, providing moorage for the float houses rocking in the marinas beside the dike. Owing to the height of the dike, little of the waterway is visible from River Road as it winds westward from downtown Ladner. In 1.8 mi. (3 km) it passes the bridge over Canoe Passage that links Ladner with Westham Island and the George C. Reifel Migratory Bird Sanctuary; 1.5 mi. (2.5 km) farther the road ends in a gated cul-de-sac. There is parking here.

As you climb up onto the gravel-surfaced dike trail the mouth of Canoe Passage presents itself all at once. The channel is several hundred metres across at this point. The flat farmland of Westham Island lies demurely on the opposite shore, a stubby red silo sticking out above its furrowed fields like the proverbial sore thumb.

The dike trail is wide enough so that walkers, bike riders and those on horseback can share it with ease. Several weathered barns, nearly colourless except for their moss-green roofs, sit with their floorboards prudently raised off the ground just in case of any breach in the dike. Wildlife—foxes, owls, swallows—claim the barns as their own now. Thick hedges of blackberry brambles ring the barns. A tall stand of Lombardy poplars planted long ago provides some shade; otherwise the land is wide open, with only an occasional willow for relief.

Old pilings march out into the Fraser from the river's edge like stalwart centurions, the last of a legion that once supported the Brunswick Cannery wharf, one of the Fraser River's earliest salmon canneries. The marsh ground at the point is usually wet, so if you want to explore out here, bring some rubber boots. One of the best times for this is midsummer, when much of the marsh is in bloom. Driftwood stranded above the high-tide line by winter storms provides natural bridges to clamber over. Some trunks are weathered smooth and curved just right for sitting back on while listening for bird calls. Don't forget your binoculars, or your paint box if you're so inclined. It's calm out here on a good day and there aren't usually more than a handful of others with whom to share the trail.

From this starting point the trail swings south in a gentle curve around Roberts Bank towards the superport causeway and the Tsawwassen ferry terminal, an easy hour's walk one way and half that on a bicycle. Viewpoints occur at regular intervals, with a bench or two set off beside the trail.

A drainage ditch separates the dike trail from nearby fields. In early spring, when there is very little plant life to contrast with the brown earth, what colour there is comes from the reflection of the blue sky in pools of water trapped in furrowed rows.

At any time of year the view west over the Strait of Georgia is compelling, an enormous seascape of ever-changing light and dark. This is the panorama you dream of longingly when cooped up in the city.

Offshore in the shallow waters of the strait, flocks of ducks and geese bob along. Depending on the direction of the wind, they take shelter on either side of the long causeway that runs out to the loading dock where ocean freighters take on coal. A hundred black railway cars sit motionless in a line while the quiet drumming of a half-dozen diesel engines harnessed in tandem carries across the water towards the dike. There is a trail running along the causeway that juts out into Roberts Bank. This little diversion can easily add another half-hour of exploration time to the journey. When you look shoreward from out here Ladner is eerily remote. Mount Baker and other peaks in the Cascade Mountains rise up to the east. Southward, a large B.C. Ferry heads off towards Vancouver Island. A freighter is silhouetted against the shores of the Gulf Islands, with the peaks of

Vancouver Island's mountains rising above Nanaimo to the west.

The dike continues south past the causeway towards Point Roberts. A gateway to the Tsawwassen Indian Reserve bars access beyond here. By now it's time to turn around anyway and head back to Ladner.

Returning to Ladner after time spent out on top of the dike is like returning from a sailing trip. The water has been expansive and ever-present. Soon you are back on sheltered land with the horizon closing in on all sides, but you come away with a feeling of inner tranquillity and silent thanks to the dike builders for allowing you to get away for a few hours.

If you'd care to find out more about the building of the dike, visit the Delta Museum and Archives back in town at 4858 Delta Street, one block west of Elliott. The museum is in the restored 1912 Tudor-style building that once housed the Delta municipal offices (now located in more modern quarters on Highway 17).

27 | POINT ROBERTS

Go ahead. Get away to Point Roberts. Just one thing: leave your car behind. Walk, cycle, jog, but treat yourself to a visit, for once, without the automobile. Driving through Point Roberts is just too much of a cliché, but if you have to, drive slowly. Enjoy yourself on these Whatcom County back roads. To find your way to this little bit of Washington, take Highway 99 south through the Massey Tunnel to the Highway 17 South exit. Turn left off Highway 17 South to Tsawwassen on Point Roberts Road and follow it to the Canada-U.S. border. You can leave your car on Wallace Avenue on the Canadian side and cycle or walk from here.

Many visitors to the tiny American enclave adjoining Tsawwassen might have problems thinking of Point Roberts as more than a giant gas station. But it has long been a magnet for Canadians, attracting visitors from the Lower Mainland for more than a half-century. The famous borderline that demarcates the modest peninsula from east to west is celebrated by a stone marker laid in 1861 under the terms of the Treaty of Washington.

To find the monument, turn right onto Roosevelt Way immediately after crossing the border. Make your way the short distance to the western end of the road before it veers sharply south. The earlier in the year you go the less likely you are to tangle with the brambles that thrive in the area around the small obelisk. There is an inscription on each side of the monument. A rough trail next to it runs along the bluff beneath a stand of old-growth Douglas fir, sculpted by the wind. Far below, the waters of the Strait of Georgia lap the beach, and the jetties of

View from Point Roberts

the Tsawwassen ferry causeway and the Roberts Bank coal facility jut into view.

Don't bother trying to make your way down the slippery slope here. Several minutes farther south along the road is a much more hospitable approach to the sea.

There are certain cardinal dates on the calendar that draw many of us out into the countryside in celebration. The summer and winter solstices are two that come to mind. I've spent both—on different years—in Lighthouse Park. No, not the well-known park in West Vancouver with rocky cliffs and tall forest, but its far more modest counterpart just south of the obelisk on the southwestern tip of Point Roberts, where the wind sweeps over sand dunes as the surf rattles agate pebbles on the beach.

Along the way to Lighthouse Park, on Marine Drive, you pass the Reef and the Breakers taverns. Before Expo 86 brought about a relaxation of the Sunday drinking laws in B.C., these American establishments lent a certain besotted exoticism to visits to this territorial anomaly.

Lighthouse Park is part of the Whatcom County parks system. In recent years it has grown beyond being a simple beach destination, and now a series of boardwalks and trails run through the dunes next to the parking lot. Stunted pines with a bonsai look and wild rose bushes thick with fat red and brown rosehips help anchor the dunes. Fire rings are located in the shelter of some of them.

As the park's summer popularity has increased, Whatcom County has introduced a small fee for park users, with extra charges if you arrive with a boat or wish to stay overnight. During three seasons of the year there's no one to bother you about paying the fee, one of several reasons I like visiting this park at off-peak times.

There's a special resonance here at the spring or fall equinox and the winter or summer solstice. Set back off the beach on the west side of the park is a tusk-shaped slab of polished black granite. Known as the Sunsweep sculpture, this small installation is one of three such markers placed along the Canada-U.S. border as part of an international art project. The other two are at Roosevelt-Campobello Park in New Brunswick and on American Point Island in Ontario's Lake of the Woods Park. Inscribed on the base of the Boundary Bluff marker are these words:

> Aligned to the north star, solstices and equinoxes, [Sunsweep] portrays the path of the sun from east to west. Designed by David Barr in 1985 and given to the people of this community as a symbol of international friendship.

Unfortunately, vandals seem to have missed the point of Barr's gesture. The tusk has been broken in two, but willing hands have glued it back together and it stands in place once more, less vaunted but undaunted, facing Vancouver Island in the western distance and Mount Baker rising above the waters of Semiahmoo Bay in the east.

Here at land's end, grand views of Haro, Juan de Fuca and Georgia straits open up on three sides. Winds and countervailing currents swirl against each other, encouraging the water into playful surf. At sea level, only the northern exposure is concealed behind the dunes—a good thing, as that is where the signs of Shell, Exxon and Chevron line Tyee Drive. Out on the beach, a modest breakwater of wooden pilings valiantly but vainly tries to hold back the surf rolling toward the lighthouse (which, in this case, is less of a house and more of a metal scaffolding).

Perched inland a short distance from the beach, a three-storey observation tower rises above a small interpretive centre. Profiles of three pods of orca whales—80 in number—that frequent the waters off the point from May to October are presented on murals. The distinctive dorsal fin markings of some of the older pod members are shown in the exhibit. Using these as clues, visitors fortunate enough to sight the whales can positively identify individuals such as one named Sealth, who is at least 31 years old.

No tour of Point Roberts would be complete without a visit to Maple Beach on the east side of the point, close to the border. From Lighthouse Park, follow Edwards Drive as it curves around the marina to meet A.P.A. Road. Follow A.P.A. east and turn north on Boundary Bay Road, a 10-minute ride by bicycle over mostly level terrain. Near the road's north end there's a good viewpoint in several directions across the wide curve in Boundary Bay's perimeter. Mountains on the North Shore vie with Mount Baker for attention. As the road descends to Bayview Drive you get a good look at Maple Beach below, while passing one of Point Roberts's oldest farm homesteads, recently restored to its former glory, on the west side.

Maple Beach still sports a few decaying pylons from the time when there was a large pier here where ship passengers would disembark. Though the pier and the tourists are gone, the beach retains its charm, especially as a spot to view a full moon rising behind Mount Baker. If you're looking for an open vantage point for stargazing, Lighthouse Park and Maple Beach are ideal locations. There is far less artificial light dulling the night sky's natural blackness here than nearby in areas of denser population. As for swimming in Boundary Bay, you'll find the water at Maple Beach is decidedly warmer than at Lighthouse Point.

When you're ready to head for home, you can either cross on the beach or head west on Roosevelt Way to the U.S. and Canadian customs stations on Tyee Drive.

THE GULF ISLANDS

INSTANT ISLAND-HOPPING

Island-hopping isn't exclusive to far-away places in the Caribbean or Micronesia. A look through the B.C. Ferries schedule reveals an amazing combination of connections between five of the southern Gulf Islands: Galiano, Mayne, Pender, Saturna and Saltspring. If you're really in the mood to rack up memories from as many as possible, you can tack on Thetis, Kuper and Gabriola islands, too.

Travelling as a foot passenger, with or without a bike or boat, is one way to attempt the feat of hopping between as many ports as possible, but you have to be light on your toes and have a bit of luck on your side to make some of the sailings. Sheer volume tends to skew the arrivals and departures schedule, especially on weekends, though connecting ferries do wait for each other once you reach the islands.

And the price is right: currently just over $10 for a trip between Tsawwassen or Horseshoe Bay and one of the southern Gulf Islands, with a small additional charge to move between islands once you're there. It's extra to travel with a bike, kayak or canoe. You cannot actually buy a round-trip ticket, but instead pay each time you board a ferry. Don't be alarmed when you're asked to pay more when travelling west of Tsawwassen—the return fare is only half as much. Get it? Never mind—even B.C. Ferries employees have trouble with the logic.

Gulf Island getaways are in a class by themselves. Each island is like a little country of its own, with a unique history and personality worth discovering and exploring. Don't push it by trying too much in one visit. Pick an island and try it out. With

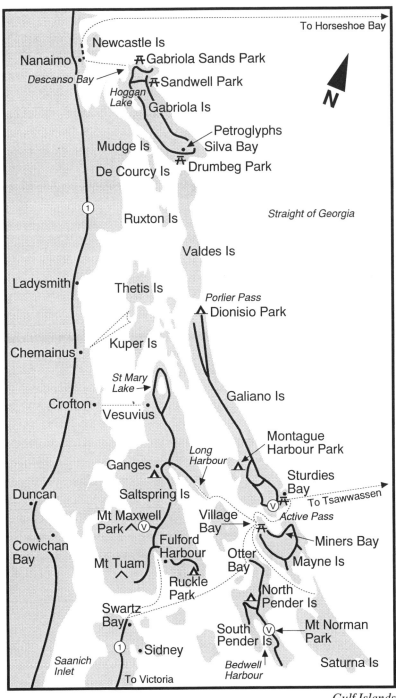

Gulf Islands

Viewpoint on South Pender

that experience tucked away in your memory bank you'll have a foundation on which to build future getaways. As for timing, it's hard to resist visiting when the weather's hot and sunny, about a third of the calendar year, but don't overlook the remaining eight months. There are hauntingly beautiful times around the Christmas season when many island homes are decorated with coloured lights that glimmer in the fog, and fall days when rock outcroppings are glazed with frost, and spring mornings when the scent of the earth awakening perfumes the air. An island's isolated nature lends a special poignancy to such occasions, perhaps because the pulse rate of a thousand-person community—about average for most islands, with Saltspring being the exception—allows more room for natural resonances that are drowned out when you raise that count to a million.

28 | MAYNE ISLAND

Here's an island really worthy of a day trip: not too big, not too small, perfectly situated and equally well shaped. You can easily explore Mayne Island in several hours, leaving plenty of time to relax at any number of secluded—and scenic—hideaways. Although Mayne has only one public park, you'll find five public beaches to choose from. Several of the 11 local bed and breakfasts have unsurpassed reputations for excellence, and accommodations include the province's oldest continuously operated hotel. Such is the spell of Mayne Island that you may wish to pack an overnight bag, just in case.

Mayne was the original community centre for the southern Gulf Islands and was once the social hub, quaintly nicknamed Little Hell because of the tolerance accorded public consumption of alcohol by its citizenry—the other islands in the gulf chain were "dry." The lighthouse at Mayne's northern tip was erected more then a century ago. Many of the buildings in Miners Bay date from the same period, including the Springwater Lodge, where you may later find yourself keeping company with a microbrewery's finest as part of a long-standing island tradition.

But first, accomplish the task of circling the island. This is best done on a bicycle, and I've geared this chapter towards those on two wheels. There's no need to rule out bringing your car, though this quadruples the cost of a visit and denies you the opportunity of slowing down to a more leisurely island pace—much of the joy of coming across as a foot passenger. The choice is yours, and circumstances will dictate how you arrange your visit.

153

Most of the other Gulf Islands are long, skinny strips of land, but Mayne is somewhat circular, more like an amoeba in shape. Six major bays make inroads on its circumference at neat intervals. For the day tripper, there's just enough distance between each to provide a break before taking up the journey once more. The same can be said of the hills, although there are few tough climbs and mostly an equitable balance between ascents and descents. Many of the roads are shaded throughout the day, with the exception of those on the south coast, where open fields testify that farming was once the calling that brought many of the early settlers to Mayne. Overall riding time around the island is about five hours (easily half that by car).

Fresh water is a rare roadside commodity on all Gulf Islands, so you should conserve your resources. Places where you can top up your canteen include the public day-use park at Dinner Bay near the ferry terminal and several commercial locations in Miners Bay. Finding these places is not difficult. If you haven't already picked up a map of the island aboard the ferry that brought you to Mayne, get an island guide at the real-estate office next to the terminal as soon as you dock.

At first, it's difficult to judge the scale of the distances between points on the map, but the short ride from the ferry dock at Village Bay to the historic settlement at Miners Bay helps put them in perspective. Once you've climbed up from the ferry dock onto Village Bay Road it's mostly downhill heading clockwise around to Miners Bay. On your left as you go is the Helen Point Indian reserve, standing in tranquil contrast to development elsewhere on the island.

Miners Bay is truly Mayne's centre, anchored by the Springwater Lodge beside the federal wharf. The lodge started life as the Collinson family's boarding house, was upgraded to the Grandview Lodge in the 1910s and only later became the Springwater. In continuous operation for all this time, it now vies with the Lund Hotel on the Sunshine Coast for the distinction of being the oldest in B.C. You can still get a meal, a drink and, if needed, a bed at the Springwater. Flanking it for several blocks are numerous period homes with lovingly tended gardens, some of which also offer lodging in the old Mayne Island spirit. A garage, several grocery and hardware stores, a bakery and an agency liquor store make Miners Bay an indispensable place to begin (and end) a visit to Mayne. Take some time to

Tinkerer's Retreat bed and breakfast

explore before moving on. If you're here in July or August, visit
the former jail that now houses the Mayne Island Museum, open
from 11 A.M. to 3 P.M. Friday to Sunday. It's two blocks up
Fernhill Road from the Springwater, across from the agricultural
hall.

Once you've done Miners Bay and have stocked up on provisions for the rest of the journey, head east along Georgina
Point Road. Take a few minutes to sit on the bench beneath the
pointed archway below the hill on which St. Mary Magdalene
Anglican Church presides over 4 acres (1.6 ha) gifted by Saturna
Island pioneer and frontier legend Warburton Pike. There's a
good view of Active Pass from here, framed by nature. The 1898
church is picturesque and worth a look inside if you're passing
on a Sunday. The baptismal font is a curiosity: a naturally carved
sandstone basin brought over in a rowboat from Saturna Island
in 1900. The pulpit has seen a lot of fire and brimstone pour
forth, though that's not the way it's done any longer.

One thing visitors learn quickly about the roads on Mayne is
to anticipate a hill climb at the beginning of each leg of the
journey. This is then followed by a long, smooth stretch where
the wind whistles through the vents in your helmet. One of the
toughest hill climbs occurs just east of Miners Bay. As Georgina

Point Road passes homesteads and gardens overlooking Active Pass, your heart may momentarily sink as you wonder how much of the island is as steep as this hill. Try it early in the day, while you still have lots of steam. You may have to dismount and push for a short distance to the top before gliding at ever-increasing speed towards the lighthouse on the point. The ride from Miners Bay to Georgina Point will take only 20 minutes but several of those minutes will seem much longer than others.

Visiting hours at the lighthouse are 1 to 3 P.M. daily: at other times the gate is closed. The Active Pass lighthouse is manned by a keeper who also has a reputation as an accomplished carver in the Haida tradition. (If you come by too early to meet him, or to have a look out at the ocean from the lighthouse, you can still check out the scenery near the point by following Bayview south off Georgina Point Road and taking the first left to its end.)

Continue on along Waugh Road towards Campbell Bay, another short ride. For the boat launch and beach at David Cove turn left off Waugh Road onto Porter, then take the first left again on Petrus to its end.

Like many of the bays on the island, Campbell Bay has public beach access but is not well marked. Watch for a shady trail that runs straight down the embankment, with the ocean at the bottom, as you round the bay on the road. This is a good spot to picnic in the cover of the overhanging forest, with the broad bay spread before you and a swath of pebble beach stretching out on each side. The beach is backed with well-worn driftwood logs mired to their knots—perfect backrests, shaded from the elements by the overhanging salmonberry and huckleberry bushes. This is a great destination for kids, who can explore the intricately carved sandstone cliffs on the bay's north side where it stretches out towards Edith Point. The uninterrupted view from the beach is due south across the Strait of Georgia towards Vancouver.

If you're journeying with younger family members, this may be as far as you want or need to come. Certainly you will be tempted to linger as you sit in the shade admiring the cascading vines of wild ocean spray with their delicate, white flowering cones.

It's uphill once more south of Campbell Bay, but your stop

on the beach should have recharged your tanks, so bear down.

At the junction of Campbell Bay Road and Fernhill your choice is to either head back north to Miners Bay or go south to Bennett or Horton bays. There's a good beach at Bennett Bay but not at Horton. To reach Bennett Bay follow Fernhill left where it divides with Horton Bay Road. There are several points of beach access from Arbutus Drive. The Mayne Inn is a convenient place in which to stop and wet your whistle, clean your plate and refill your canteen. Formerly called the Arbutus Lodge, it was originally built to house workers at a proposed brickyard on Bennett Bay. Financial trouble kept the plan from ever coming to fruition.

Fresh shrimp and crab are available at the federal dock in Horton Bay every day from 4 to 6 P.M., the one drawing card for venturing down the Horton Bay Road to its end. Surprisingly, fresh seafood for sale is often difficult to find on the Gulf Islands, and it takes a dockside connection to make it happen. Watch for a truck parked at the wharf with the personalized licence plate reading "CRAB 4U"—that's your contact.

To complete a circle tour of Mayne Island, continue right on Gallagher Bay Road as it turns south off Horton Bay Road. You now enter the fertile heartland of the island, where the farming of tomatoes and daffodils was a major success story in the 1930s and early 1940s. Apples, chickens, sheep, even dried seaweed (*nori* or *hijiki* for the Japanese market) have been successfully exported by Mayne Island producers. Today the island imports most of these items; its one remaining export is raw logs.

There is a public beach at Piggott Bay and another at Dinner Point Community Park, though the west side of Mayne overlooking Navy Channel has nothing to rival the beauty of Campbell or Bennett bays. Dinner park has water, changing rooms and a fair to middling beach. What it has also featured in recent years has been an annual ukulele concert by schoolchildren from both Mayne and the Hawaiian islands as part of an exchange program. In the summer, when soft winds blow warm off Active Pass, your active imagination would be forgiven for hearing strains of ukuleles carried on the air, caught by the trees and pinned to an overhead arbutus branch by the breeze.

The last push takes you around to Village Bay on Dinner Road and then Dalton Drive before linking up with Village Bay Road. Village Bay's altogether modern appearance stands in particular contrast to the heritage look of nearby Miners Bay.

Time now to sprint back to Miners Bay for a last visit to the Springwater before returning to catch your ferry home. One brief visit to Mayne Island is enough to bring you back for a longer stay, and well it should. Mayne has no public campground, but it boasts more highly rated bed and breakfasts (featuring, in many cases, much more than breakfast) than any other Gulf Island. There are homes to suit a wide range of budgets, from the modest Tinkerer's Retreat to the Victorian charm of the Gingerbread House. Only the Tinkerer's Retreat (539-2280) offers guests the use of bicycles, so bring your own, as at present there is neither a bicycle shop nor a rental outlet on Mayne.

29 | SALTSPRING ISLAND

Welcome to the fat cat of the Gulf Islands. Because Saltspring is the biggest, most populous of all—as well as possessed of the most poetic name—its pace is busy for a Gulf Island, but you're still a world away from city life. Quietly riding along with no one to rush you, pausing beside a government wharf to sniff the air, exploring a heritage farm where trails lead down to the sea—this is Saltspring Island. Because it lies in the rain shadow of the Vancouver Island Ranges, Saltspring enjoys as much sunshine as the Okanagan and only half the yearly precipitation that falls on Vancouver. This makes it an ideal all-season destination for day trippers. With eight parks, five gas stations, two bank machines, one liquor store and a marriage commissioner, almost anyone can have a good time here.

By the very nature of its size, Saltspring provides opportunities for more sightseeing than you can easily fit into a one-day visit. If you're looking to get a feel for the island's soul, there are two provincial parks on the southern half of the island that are must-sees: Mount Maxwell Provincial Park for its lofty views and Ruckle Provincial Park for its heritage seaside perspective.

The ferry that brings you to Saltspring from Vancouver arrives at Long Harbour. If you were to imagine a pterodactyl's head in profile, you wouldn't be far off the shape of the upper third of the island's body, which is made up of three distinct sections, and in anatomical terms possesses a head, thorax and abdomen. (Nature does some strange things out here.) Long Harbour is well inside the creature's long mouth.

(If you happen to be travelling from Swartz Bay on Vancouver Island, the ferry arrives at Fulford Harbour on the island's south side. Yet a third ferry to Saltspring sails from Crofton, also on Vancouver Island, and lands at Vesuvius Bay, on a neck of land a short distance west of Ganges and the site of the island's first modern-day settlement in the summer of 1859.)

The Athol Peninsula juts out like a pincer into Trincomali Channel, with Galiano Island to the east and Prevost Island much closer to the southeast. The ferry from Vancouver makes its way up into Long Harbour between Nose and Scott points.

Upon arrival, there is a rush of disembarking ferry traffic north on Long Harbour Road, which skirts the east side of Ganges Harbour as it goes. Try not to get caught up in this frenzy. Pull over and get your feet on the ground beside the ferry dock. There's even a little picnic area at the beach across from the ferry on Welbury Bay. Put down some roots. See if you can spot a seal or two bobbing up curiously among the kelp beds. Sniff the salt air, get into the island groove. Don't let the cars dashing from Long Harbour fool you: it's much more laid-back here than the traffic implies.

There is also beach access almost immediately to the east of Long Harbour Road if you follow Peregrine Road to either Ontario Beach, via Quebec Drive, or Beachside Drive where there is better picnicking.

Long Harbour Road leads northwest to the central island town of Ganges, today the commercial hub of Saltspring Island. Among the earliest industries on the island was a sandstone quarry in nearby Vesuvius. (Like Ganges, Vesuvius was named after a Royal Navy vessel.) One of the quarry's first customers was the City of Victoria, which wanted sidewalk slabs to line the streets. The U.S. Federal Mint in San Francisco, constructed later in the century, was also a major account.

Tucked into the hillside on the west side of Ganges is Mouat Provincial Park, a wooded camping area with 15 sites just a short walk from the centre of town. This park, created in 1961 on a gift of land from Saltspring's well-known Mouat family, provides little more than a base from which to explore the island but it serves this purpose well. You can walk to dinner in minutes at one of Ganges's fine restaurants and toddle back when you're done! Follow the signs from the centre of town to locate the park.

Mount Maxwell viewpoint to Fulford Harbour

Ganges is large enough to compel you to stop. Older wooden buildings arranged around the waterfront convey the weathered flavour of years past. The gas station here closes at 6 P.M. A liquor store is also located here, though in the midst of all the commercial activity that abounds in Ganges it's harder to locate than on other islands. Now *that's* big-time.

Heading south, it's 8 mi. (13 km) from Ganges to Fulford Harbour where the island constricts again. With the road rising, falling and curving much of the way along the Fulford-Ganges Road, you're in for a fun ride if you've come by bicycle. Make sure you've got liquid refreshment with you, as there are few services along the way.

MOUNT MAXWELL PROVINCIAL PARK   Watch for Cranberry Road leading west from the Fulford-Ganges Road. Signs help point the way to Mount Maxwell, Saltspring's first provincial park. Cranberry Road feeds into Maxwell Road, and the climb from here to the top of the mountain is quite challenging; not much has been done to improve road conditions since the park opened in 1938. Just before you reach the summit the road passes through a stand of elegant old growth—grand fir and Garry oak—that has been set aside as an ecological reserve.

161

From the top of Mount Maxwell the whole of the valley below on the south end of Saltspring is revealed, running across the island from Fulford Harbour to Burgoyne Bay (named for the captain of the *Ganges*). With luck you'll arrive on a clear day when you can survey the other Gulf Islands, Vancouver Island and the San Juans, capped off by the always astonishing sight of Mount Baker rising above the plains of western Washington. Mind your step up here, as a series of cliffs drop straight down the south face of Mount Maxwell. Venturing out on them is dangerous even with the proper climbing equipment, but there are a number of safe locations near the viewpoint here on Baynes Peak at the top of Mount Maxwell. Pick a ledge on which to stretch out for a picnic or to soak up some rays in the shelter of the stone walls. You may be treated to an aerial display by groups of ravens catching updrafts off the face of the mountain. Hang-gliders are similarly inspired. Although it isn't the highest peak on Saltspring (that distinction rests on the shoulder of Bruce Peak to the south), Mount Maxwell combines easy accessibility with one of the best views of any on the Gulf Islands. There are numerous hiking trails here, many of them quite old and not all that well marked.

(There's also hiking on Mount Tuam and on Bruce Peak. From Fulford Harbour you can take Musgrave Road to reach them both, though eventually by different trails leading north off Musgrave to Bruce and south to Tuam. You'll find great views from both down onto the Saanich Inlet and peninsula, and across Satellite Channel to Cowichan Bay.)

Heading south from Mount Maxwell park on the Fulford-Ganges Road now allows you to enjoy the rolling farmland you've glimpsed from above. Owing to the island's geological history, there is surprisingly little fallow ground on Saltspring, but despite this deficiency many settlers tried scratching a living from the soil. Some made out better than others, particularly those who were able to clear land around Fulford Harbour and on the island's north end. They may have had to work harder than pioneers on more fertile islands such as Mayne and Pender, but they had as their reward one of the most beautiful natural settings of all. You can certainly appreciate this while you make your way south to Fulford Harbour. There's little evidence of commercial activity around the harbour, but nearby on Beaver

Point Road is the community hall, where activities of a cultural kind, namely music and dancing, are held regularly.

The Fulford-Ganges Road ends when it reaches Fulford Harbour, where two new roads originate, branching south and east. The road south and west is Musgrave Road; the eastern route leads to Beaver Point and Ruckle Provincial Park.

Drummond Regional Park is on Fulford Harbour a short distance south on Musgrave Road. This is a day-use-only park, featuring a seaside beach, a children's playground and an uncommon petroglyph boulder, perhaps a remnant from an ancient native community once located on the shores of Fulford Harbour. A resident of this settlement may have carved the image that graces the stone a millennium or two ago. With eyes of concentric circles that stare back hypnotically at observers, and a gaping mouth that looks hungry for sustenance, the face on the boulder presents a riveting image, as though the carver is looking straight through the walls of time at us today. The petroglyph is one of two identified on Saltspring; the other is on a private beach at Parminter Point on the island's upper west side.

RUCKLE PROVINCIAL PARK A popular concept of the early settlement of Canada by Europeans has them arriving on the Atlantic coast and steadily spreading westward across the land. While this is largely true, certain impatient settlers couldn't wait. Long before the Canadian Pacific Railway was built, they came on ahead by boat via the Pacific, some intending to seek their fortune in the Cariboo gold rush and others to establish present-day Victoria at the invitation of colonial governor James Douglas. By the 1850s several groups of settlers had moved to Saltspring with the intention of farming. A mixed bunch, their numbers included tapped-out miners returning from the Cariboo who had originally arrived from Australia, plus a group of black American families Douglas invited north from California to escape discrimination. (Although there had been permanent native communities on some of the other Gulf Islands, Saltspring was used on a purely seasonal basis by the Indians travelling from their home bases on Vancouver Island.)

Among the new arrivals were Henry Ruckle and his young son Daniel. Together they put down roots on Saltspring Island's southern tip, establishing the province's first family farm in

The old Ruckle homestead

1872—or so says the information posted by B.C. Parks on the Ruckle property. Members of the family are still working 200 acres (80 ha) of cleared, rolling land surrounding the original buildings. Apple orchards dominate in places, testimony that this was a profitable crop for the Ruckles long before the Okanagan Valley opened up. Produce was shipped to markets in Victoria and New Westminster from nearby Fulford Harbour. Generations of sheep have been keeping the ground below the trees free of windfalls; they still manicure the green growth in nearby pastures.

In June of 1974, a transfer agreement was reached whereby the provincial government received property from the Ruckle family to be used as public parkland. In the subsequent years, the 5.5-mi. (9-km) road from Fulford Harbour has been paved and now presents an easy 30-minute ride by bicycle.

Saltspring Island is the most popular Gulf Island with travellers, especially during summer months, and Ruckle is the largest park on any of these islands; as such, it draws a considerable number of visitors every year. One of the interesting features here is that the 80 campsites are of the walk-in rather than drive-in variety. (There is parking for RVs but no campsites immediately adjacent.) Short trails run from a series of parking lots to Beaver Point where there are individual and group campsites on cleared embarkments next to the ocean. You can lie in your tent at night and watch the ferries passing, lit up like floating hotels. Most of the 5 mi. (8 km) of shoreline around the park is sloping rock, with only one major beach (on the bay in front of the Ruckle farm).

Ruckle is a surprising park in many ways. Arriving visitors enter what looks like a working farm. Vintage wooden buildings dot the clearing, including a beautifully preserved Queen Anne-style home still occupied by George Ruckle and his family. There are descriptive markers, some with historic photos, affixed to each building. It's easy to see how the spread grew from the original farmhouse to include a building for every use: creamery, chicken coop, machine shop, barn and a host of other buildings served the farm. All have been surprisingly well maintained. The cream-yellow paint on the old house and the reds on the barn wall have weathered so that in autumn they blend perfectly with the seasonal shades of the surrounding forest.

Another surprise is the tall stands of original Douglas fir, arbutus and Garry oak ringing the property. As you might expect on a century-old farm, trails lead off in many directions under the shelter of the forest. One long path leads from the orchards down to a small bay, where one of the island's best public beaches lies. Find a log to prop yourself on while you marvel at the marine activity out in Swanson Channel. North Pender Island lies directly across the waves. From the bay, a long winding path leads through the forest beside the ocean to the campsites, beach and picnic areas. You can ride your bike for much of the distance, and walk it over the rockier stretches.

Pieces of curled arbutus bark litter the forest floor like a scattering of cinnamon sticks. The size of the trees is breathtaking, and their shaping by salt spray suggests the strength of winter storms.

Ruckle park is ideally suited for visits by bicycle. Weekends in late fall or early spring are great times to ride to Ruckle park. It might be raining in Vancouver, but chances are that you can find relief on rustic Saltspring.

A note on the spelling of the island's name: according to tradition, the name is two words, Salt Spring, which dates back to the 19th century. Saltspring was originally known as Chuan Island in the late 1700s when it was first surveyed by the Royal Navy, then was renamed Admiral Island in 1859. Over the following five decades it becomes better known as "Salt Spring," an appellation stemming from a series of natural brine springs at the island's north end. In 1905, when the Geographic Board of Canada conducted a study of place names across the country, they decided to err on the side of simplicity by tidying all these double-barrelled place names into one-word forms. B.C.'s current provincial toponymist, Janet Mason, whose job it is to decide such matters, is not sure if the decision was right or wrong, or truly reflected island opinion, but in any case Salt Spring became Saltspring. Long-time residents of the island still spell it with two names as a way in which to differentiate themselves from more recent arrivals. Mason has corresponded with a variety of island groups, such as the chamber of commerce and the publisher of the island's newspaper, the *Driftwood*, and continues to find opinion divided on which usage is preferable. Meanwhile, efforts on the part of B.C. Ferries in its printed schedules, as well as Canada Post's signage at the two post offices on Saltspring, to spell the name as two words are looked on by Mason as misguided, not to mention misinformed.

30 | GALIANO ISLAND

Galiano Island has a century-old reputation as a leisuretime destination. It's a fact of life (and nature) that there's always been more money on Galiano in tourism than in farming. Count heads and you'll find people outnumber sheep by a much wider margin here than on any other Gulf Island. Island businesses also cater more to outdoors pursuits, such as ocean kayaking and mountain biking. Three provincial parks complement two equally impressive community land trusts. Forest-lined roadways lead to white sand and shell beaches. Sheltered waters welcome boaters, and back roads beckon cyclists. You can come prepared for just about anything—and find it here.

Three hundred years after Columbus's most famous voyage, the British and Spanish fleets were playing peekaboo with each other along the B.C. coast. Their common objective was to explore new territory, laying claim to it for their respective monarchs. Galiano Island was caught in the crossfire of this competitive name game and, as a result, English and Spanish place names vie for importance along its shoreline and promontories.

It must have come as something of a surprise to the Coast Salish who had lived around a fertile bay on the island for millennia to discover that they were, henceforth, residents of Montague Harbour (named for a British ship and now part of a provincial park), located next to Sutil Mountain (named for Captain Galiano's schooner). Active Pass, at Galiano's south end, was named by the British for an American paddle steamer; Porlier Pass at its north end was named for a bureaucrat in Madrid. What a tussle.

Galiano is divided into two separate administrative jurisdictions; most islanders live on the southern half. There's more to this split than simple satisfaction of organizational needs. Indeed, when you talk with islanders they'll point to a difference in lifestyle at each end. Where those on North Galiano are more likely to value their solitude, residents in the south are more active socially, though taken as a whole Galiano's community is one of the most artistic and environmentally progressive in the Gulf Islands.

In geological terms, Galiano is far younger than the other Gulf Islands, though superficially their features are the same. Galiano has very little land suitable for agriculture and thus was one of the last islands to be settled by Europeans and Asians. By force of sheer geography, much of the population is confined to the southern third of the land mass.

Almost as soon as you disembark from the ferry at Sturdies Bay, you are in the heart of a small commercial district, one of two such gathering spots on the island. Galiano's only gas station is just uphill, across Sturdies Bay Road from the visitor information booth. Unlike the self-serve booth, which features a variety of literature about the island, the gas station and most businesses close at 5 or 6 P.M. The government outlet liquor store (uphill from the gas station and next to the Trincomali Bakery) closes at 5, leaving off-sales from the Hummingbird Pub, farther along Porlier Pass Road in the other commercial district, as your only other option. Next to the gas station is Gulf Island Kayaking (539-2442), which offers year-round exploration of the island by water. The Dandelion Gallery, featuring work by island artists, is also nestled into this little intersection. Two grocery stores, a craft gallery and the post office are a short distance farther up island at the intersection of Porlier Pass and Georgeson Bay roads.

It's 22 mi. (35 km) from Sturdies Bay to Dionisio Point Provincial Park at the island's north end, quite a stretch for those on bicycles—it will take four to five hours to cover the undulating road on two wheels, less than an hour on four. Although there is little likelihood of losing your way, as Porlier Pass Road is the only one that runs the full length of the island, there are numerous activities closer to Sturdies Bay to occupy a day trip. As you move around the island clockwise, an enjoyable procession of parks and viewpoints present themselves for exploration.

Rock formations at Bellhouse Provincial Park

Bellhouse Provincial Park, Montague Harbour Provincial Marine Park, Mount Galiano and Bluffs Park are all within easy range of the ferry terminal.

Since there's more to do in a day than you can fit in one visit, plan in advance whether you'll come with a car or on foot, riding a bike or pulling a boat. You can often arrange to rent equipment, such as a kayak or a mountain bike, and have it waiting for you when you arrive. Pick the right bed and breakfast and they may supply the equipment for you as part of your stay. Anything's possible on Galiano.

BELLHOUSE PROVINCIAL PARK   As soon as you're past the commercial district near the terminal, turn left off Sturdies Bay Road onto Burrill Road, following the sign pointing to Bellhouse Provincial Park. Turn left again onto Jack Drive and go to its end. You'll be surprised at how quickly you can reach this park, making it an immediate reward at the start of your visit.

Bellhouse has been a public day-use site since 1964 when it was deeded to the province by the family of the same name, who have resided at Burrill Point since 1904. The Bellhouses, who know a thing or two about island visitors, operated the Farmhouse Inn from the 1920s to the 1960s. Over the years guests at the inn enjoyed watching the marine traffic in Active

Pass, and it was Leonard Bellhouse's wish in bequeathing the land to the public that it should remain for this purpose. Certainly the magnificence of the park's location far outweighs its modest 5-acre (2-ha) size. A small beach lies along its eastern shoreline, while around the point on the west side are some of the most animated shapes of eroded limestone on the island. This park is a photographer's dream, both for its natural setting and for the the scale of human activity when large ferry boats churn by.

BLUFFS PARK   Whether you're driving, journeying on foot or cycling, make the next place you visit after Bellhouse be Bluffs Park, with its views from above of what you've experienced at shoreline. To reach Bluffs Park return back down Jack Drive, turning left at the junction with Burrill Road. You will pass a number of old homesteads with orchards of wizened fruit trees as the road leads west, then turns uphill onto Bluff Road. The climb from here to Bluffs Park will have you puffing in no time. As the paved road ascends, it passes beside the private cabins of Driftwood Village Resort (539-5457). Uphill from here, just off Bluff Road on Warbler Road, is Galiano Bicycle Rental and Repairs (539-2806), a good place to stop if you're in need of advice or assistance. (The owners will have a bicycle waiting at the ferry dock if you make arrangements in advance.) Matthew Schoenfeld runs the bicycle shop along with his partner, Pamela Taylor, and is also a member of the Knifemakers Guild. Ask to see samples of his handmade knives, designed for a variety of applications.

Bluff Road becomes gravel-surfaced just past Warbler Road. A large wooden sign announces that you have entered the Bluffs. Watch for a road leading off to the left about one-sixth of a mile (0.25 km) beyond this sign. It leads out to the spectacular viewpoint on the Bluffs, one of the best in the islands. From up here you can see all of Active Pass below, including Bellhouse Provincial Park on one side and Georgeson Bay to the south. The Georgesons were early settlers of the island, and you can still see the cleared fields of their homestead. They moved to Mayne Island in 1885 to become the first lighthouse keepers at Georgina Point.

Bluffs Park was made possible through a donation in 1972 of this land from Max and Marion Enke, who lived on Galiano from 1902 to 1913, then moved to Victoria. A plaque honouring their gift of 336 acres (136 ha) stands beside the parking area. Follow the trail that runs along the bluff past an old wooden shelter for the best views of Mayne, Saturna, Pender, Saltspring and Vancouver islands before descending through the woods on the loop trail to meet up with Bluff Road once more. There are numerous spots on the bluff for a picnic, but please, no fires.

If you're on a bike, make the thrilling descent down Bluff Road to Georgeson Bay Road through a tall stand of cedar trees. Don't hurtle by too quickly or you'll miss the special feeling of passing among them. On an island that's been as heavily logged as Galiano, scenes like this are rare indeed.

EASTERN FOREST ROAD   Once on Georgeson Bay Road you can return to Sturdies Bay or take Montague Harbour Road to reach the provincial park 2 mi. (3 km) distant, or explore the east side of the island on a lengthy forest road.

To find your way across to the east side, follow Georgeson Bay Road east until you reach the grocery stores and Humming-bird Pub at the intersection with Porlier Pass Road. Turn left onto Porlier, right onto Galiano Way, then left again onto Georgia View Road. From here the road leads a considerable way north to Coon Bay and Dionisio Point Provincial Park. Along the way are a number of roads that lead down to small beaches overlooking the Strait of Georgia. If you are looking for the ocean but don't want to go to the trouble of heading up island (thereby avoiding this hidden side of Galiano, with its clearcuts and massive brush piles), rather than turning on Georgia View Road continue along Galiano Way and turn left onto Sticks Allison Road. Follow a trail at the end of this road down onto the beach.

MONTAGUE PROVINCIAL MARINE PARK   If you decide to head for Montague Harbour you will discover that the sheltered west side of Galiano is much different from its exposed eastern counter-part, with far fewer signs of logging. Instead, you will be entering a narrow fertile valley that has been home to humans for thousands of years. Evidence of this can be seen in the middens—massive mounds of bleached sea shells—that cover several of the beaches and grassy areas next to the harbour.

When Montague Provincial Marine Park opened in 1959, it

was the first provincial park to cater to visitors who arrive in their own boats, as well as those who come by ferry. The sheltered harbour was the site of the B.C. Ferries dock before the operation moved to Sturdies Bay. Immediately on your left as you enter the park is the marine park and public dock. A nature house, moored beside the dock, is open during the summer. Interpretive displays of sea life and a bookstore are among its features. The beach on this side of the park is one of the better ones. On the hillside above the harbour are 15 walk-in campsites, half of which have commanding views of the water. Sites 31 to 38 are the best locations in the park. There is a small nightly charge for use of these campsites.

Farther along the road are the 25 drive-in campsites, sheltered by the forest and not exposed to the sea. From April to October there is a charge of about $15 per night for their use. Given a choice, I'd rather stay at a walk-in site. Several drive-in sites, notably 3 and 7, are reached by climbing a short set of flagstone steps. Their position above the roadway spares sleeping campers from the headlights of vehicles arriving after dark.

Farther along still, the park road brings you to the day-use picnic area, which fronts on a long curving beach. A boat-launch ramp is located next to the parking lot. The view from here up the west side of Galiano is what the Gulf Islands are all about: sheltered waterways, islands of all sizes, wildlife in the form of birds, seals and otters, boats of all kinds passing by and high cliffs that rise straight up out of the sea.

While you're exploring Montague, make sure to walk the trails that lead out onto Gray Peninsula. Ancient arbutus, Douglas fir, hemlock and Garry oak shelter thick underbrush, restricting walkers to the winding trail along the peninsula's east side. Once you're around onto the western exposure the hillside opens, beaches spread before you, and you're sure to disturb a heron as you round one of the points. Watch for one particular beach composed of ground white shells, back by an enormous midden that is being worn down more each year by the elements. No camping is allowed out here. The hour that it will take to explore the beaches and promontories of Gray Peninsula will be one of the most enjoyable of your visit to Galiano. There is a remarkable stillness waiting, with a feeling that, at last, you can stop moving for a while and just enjoy the natural rhythmn of life.

DIONISIO POINT PROVINCIAL PARK   Heading up island from
Montague Harbour is a real task if you must rely on any form of
self-propulsion. As you might realize from your visit to Montague,
before you can proceed on land you must surmount the steep cliffs
that rise above the park and continue along most of Galiano's west
side. The immediate returns are sparing: the road rises and falls
through densely wooded areas without much to enchant the eye.
(If you are approaching from Sturdies Bay, take the Porlier Pass
Road to avoid the steeper climb from Montague Harbour on
Clanton Road, which merges with Porlier at the top of the hillside
above Montague.)

North Galiano is a long 12.4 mi. (20 km) north of Montague.
At the halfway point there is a federal wharf at Retreat Cove,
and at the very north end of the island is a private one beside
the Spanish Hills General Store. Being at road's end, this place
hums with visitors in spring and summer but closes up tight in
September.

You can reach Dionisio Point Provincial Park at the island's
north end without having to travel farther than Cook Road, 4.3
mi. (7 km) north of Retreat Cove. A small blue sign points to
the right; Dionisio Point is 3 mi. (5 km) from here. Follow Cook
uphill, staying with the pavement as it passes Bodega Lodge,
and turn right where the road divides and the pavement ends.
Roadside signs inform visitors that they are passing an environmentally sensitive area that has been designated as a provincial
ecological reserve. Continue to the left as the hard-packed dirt
road meets East Side Main forestry road. Take it easy on this
last 2.2 mi. (3.5 km) to the park; enjoy the views now as your
payoff.

Dionisio Point bears the first of Captain Galiano's several
names. Logging giant MacMillan Bloedel, the major landowner
on Galiano, has for the past several years been divesting itself
of large tracts of property, creating consternation among other
property owners. As much as many residents resent the idea of
MacBlo logging any more of Galiano, they also fear overpopula-
tion and private-owner logging on an island whose water
resources are already dicey during the long, dry summer months
typical here in the Gulf Islands. Islanders have managed to
purchase Mount Galiano and Sutil Mountain from the logging
company, and they are in the process of trying to preserve
Bodega Hill, along with its unique flora and fauna.

173

Kayakers at Dionisio Point

In the midst of the controversy, the province's acquisition of Dionisio Point hasn't received much attention. For years Dionisio Point has been an unofficial camping spot—by virtue of MacMillan Bloedel turning a blind eye—at the narrow island's north end. In July of 1991, MacBlo gifted two lots of waterfront property to the province to form a Class A park at Dionisio Point. Coupled with 267 acres (108 ha) of adjacent upland that the province acquired for $830,000, the land became B.C.'s newest playground. Slightly larger than the park at Montague Harbour, Dionisio Point is an example of the public leading the way (through established land usage) and the government following.

Dionisio Point is a sandy isthmus—with a beach on each side—that stretches out towards the Strait of Georgia before branching to the north and south. The north branch of sandstone, its small cliffs and ledges topped with a thin coating of soil that supports grass cover, arbutus trees and Garry oaks, provides protection for a popular anchorage in a small cove. On the other side of the isthmus, the bare southern ridge partially encloses shallow Coon Bay, which empties completely at lowest tides. The isthmus is an ideal place to launch kayaks, canoes or car-top boats. Quietly exploring the shoreline on foot or by boat is one of the most interesting ways to spend a visit to Dionisio.

There are 15 drive-in campsites lining the shores of Coon Bay at Dionisio park and 25 walk-in sites on the hillside above. Currently there is no charge for camping here. Fresh water is available from a pump. Unfortunately, unlike at Montague Harbour, from the walk-in sites you have almost no view of the water; however, if you've made it this far by bicycle or kayak, you probably won't care all that much as long as you find a good place to pitch your tent.

The water of Porlier Pass (also known as the Cowichan Gap), running between Galiano and Valdes Island to the north, churns through at changing tide. You can actually hear the ripping sound as the surface of the pass becomes ruffled by waves and whirlpools. The only time you'd want to be out here in a small, open boat would be at slack tide. As it is, you can do almost all the exploring you wish by following the trails around to any of the four bays between Dionisio Point and the lighthouse at Race Point. Each comes out to a small point and is invested with an individual charm of its own. The red lighthouse on Boscowitz Rock and its companion nearby on Virago Point were completed in 1902.

One bonus if you do explore by water is that you won't be trespassing on the Indian reserve that encompasses Lighthouse Bay, a protected body lying between the two lights. Indian reserves are private property, posted as restricted areas, and require permission from the band office for even the lighthouse keeper to enter. No one lives on the reserve any longer, nor at the settlement visible across Porlier Pass on Valdes Island. Many former residents now live on Kuper Island to the southwest. An old Home Oil sign on the dock in Lighthouse Bay is a leftover from a time when the Indians allowed a marine service to operate in the bay for nearly two decades, but that was obviously long ago. Still, it's well worth viewing, as are the steep rock walls that line the east side of the bay. Judging from the size of the boulders on the shore and just under the surface of the water, large chunks occasionally come loose, so be careful about how close you get to the walls. A boardwalk sheltered by a stand of arbutus trees leads out from the end of the bay to the lighthouse keeper's home, allowing the keeper access to the light on Virago Point. Life out at the tip of Galiano is a secluded one. If you need help, call in at the keeper's home. Whoever is stationed here will welcome a chance to chat.

175

31 | THE PENDER ISLANDS

BOATING ◄
CAMPING ◄
CYCLING ◄
DRIVING ◄
HIKING ◄
PADDLING ◄
PICNICKING ◄
SWIMMING ◄
VIEWPOINTS ◄

Despite their apparent size, the Pender Islands are really a breeze to explore. Numerous public beaches dot the islands, in addition to a provincial campground, a provincial marine park and a regional hiking park. Getting from one to the other requires relatively little effort if you're travelling by bicycle or car. And if you're looking to the pioneer past for boating inspiration, remember that early settlers of all nationalities made their way through the channels and passes around the Penders and adjacent islands in small open boats, sometimes paying the ultimate price for their endeavours but most often journeying safely and without incident. You can tune into this age-old spirit of adventure for the price of a ferry ticket.

The Pender Islands, North and South, were once one, joined by a narrow isthmus at their middle. Their separation only served to heighten their individual identities. The actual physical act of division occurred in 1903 at the able hands of the federal government, following the request of smooth-talking local steamship operator Thomas W. Paterson (who later went on to become lieutenant-governor of B.C.).

From ancient times until this relatively recent event the Pender Island Portage (as the isthmus had been known) was part of a water and land trail network over which natives and pioneer families hauled canoes, sailboats and rowboats between Bedwell Harbour and Port Browning. By doing so they reduced the travelling time between isolated island communities considerably. The Pender Canal helped speed things up even more, though running its waters can be quite tricky at times when the tidal waters are moving. Best to attempt this one only during slack tide until you know it better!

The ferry to North Pender Island arrives at Otter Bay on the island's northwest side. Before you even set foot ashore, the view of many older homes establishes the flavour for your visit. This is an island on which to enjoy the architectural achievements of the cottage era, before the arrival of the monster home. Residents of the Pender Islands, whether summer-only or full-time, have traditionally chosen a more modest, though no less esthetically pleasing, demeanour for the design of their residences. Perhaps more here than on any other Gulf Islands (though, to be fair, this atmosphere can be found elsewhere), Pender homes reflect an assurance that cottage living can be as comfortable today as it was when the island was originally settled. Thus, a large part of the fun of visiting the Penders is just travelling slowly around the islands, admiring the layout of the homes and gardens, while musing on which one you might enjoy having for your own.

A suggestion: while making your tour, stop in at any of the 13 registered bed and breakfast locations on the island to get a feel for what they have to offer. Even if you're on the island only for the day, the hosts of each will almost invariably make time to show you their facilities in hopes that you will return to stay with them on another occasion. Several of them allow pets, several are adult-oriented. A detailed map of the B&Bs of the Pender Islands is available on all B.C. Ferries, or by calling ahead to Canadian Gulf Islands Bed & Breakfast Reservation Service, 539-5390. If you are arriving as a foot passenger with a bike or small boat and need a pick-up or drop-off while on Pender, Jeanette Campbell runs the 24-hour Pender Island Taxi, 629-9900.

The majority of homes are situated on North Pender; most of the south island is taken up by agricultural activity and woodland. Day trippers who keep this in mind can concentrate on one island or the other without trying to fit too much into one visit.

NORTH PENDER ISLAND To cyclists, particularly, it must seem inevitable that upon arrival on many islands the first challenge is an uphill climb. Such is the case for a short distance from the ferry terminal at Otter Bay to the hillside above. Once there the roadway levels out, and most of the routes around the north island present far less of a challenge. The way leads rather gently around and across the north island from one public beach and government wharf to the next, each perfectly spaced for taking breaks and breathers. There are highway signs at most intersections to direct residents and visitors alike to public-access recreation sites.

For an example of a day trip to the Pender Islands, consider the following itinerary:

Leaving Otter Bay, move clockwise in a northwestern direction around the north island, starting with a left onto Otter Bay Road, and a mile farther (about 2 km) turn left again onto Port Washington Road, following it to the federal wharf on Grimmer Bay. There's a beach to the north of the wharf. (Along the way, watch for a beach trail that leads left off Otter Bay Road, halfway between the Grimmer and Port Washington intersections. Another of these road-end beaches is just north of Port Washington at the west end of Bridges Road.) The journey over to Port Washington is a fun one because it allows you a close-up look at many of the lovely coastal homes you saw from the ferry on the way to Otter Bay.

Heading east across the island on Port Washington Road, turn left when you reach Clam Bay Road for a drive around to the government wharf at Hope Bay. The Clam Bay Road leads you there along a less travelled, more forested route in about 2 mi. (3 km). Much of the way runs past the Clam Bay Farm, with occasional views out over Navy Channel towards Mayne Island. (You can take the more direct route by simply staying on Port Washington Road.)

At Hope Bay you'll discover one of the oldest buildings on the island, the Hope Bay Heritage Store, built in 1912 to replace Corbett's Store (dated 1905 on a stained-glass remnant) when the original succumbed to a fire. Next to it on the wharf are two art galleries. Along Hope Bay from the wharf, several weathered boathouses complete the scene. This is definitely a good place to spend time with a steaming cappuccino, sitting out in front of the store under the spreading limbs of an ancient maple tree.

Heading south from Hope Bay, the road follows the shoreline. Turn right onto Hooson Road, and left soon after onto Bedwell Harbour Road. You are now heading directly south towards Otter Bay Road, which you'll meet on your left in about a third of a mile (0.5 km). Depending on your plans, and how long you've already spent exploring North Pender Island, you may

Mount Neilson lookout over Bedwell Harbour

choose to head back to the ferry on Otter Bay Road, or continue south along Bedwell Harbour Road.

Farmland embraces Bedwell Harbour Road on both sides as it leads south towards Driftwood Centre, a small mall with a variety of shops, including a B.C. liquor store and the lone gas station on the Penders.

Just south of the mall, turn east on Hamilton Road to reach the pub, marina, café and picnic ground at Hamilton Beach in Port Browning. There's also a federal wharf here. A popular port of call with boaters in the summer, Hamilton Beach is a good place to launch boats of all sizes. Look for the public ramp (no charge) at road's end to the right of the driveway leading downhill to the pub.

One suggestion for exploring Port Browning on the water is to launch here and paddle across to the public beach off Razor Point Road along the opposite shore. (There is also road access to this small beach: follow the second right turn along Razor Point Road east of Bedwell Harbour Road as you come south from Hope Bay and before you reach Driftwood Mall.)

Another possible water destination from Hamilton Beach

would be sandy Mortimer Spit at the northern mouth of the canal that links Port Browning and Bedwell Harbour.

As the main road heads south of Hamilton Road, its name changes from Bedwell Harbour Road to Canal Road even though there is no apparent difference between the two.

Prior Centennial Provincial Park, one of two public campgrounds on the Penders (and the only one with vehicle access; the other, Beaumont Provincial Marine Park on South Pender, is accessible only by water), is on the west side of Canal Road, 3.7 mi. (6 km) southeast of the ferry dock at Otter Bay. Relatively small, this 40-acre (16-ha) forested park has 17 well-spaced vehicle/tent campsites, and is a welcome resting place for those thinking of extending a day trip into an overnight affair. A self-registered fee is payable for use of the sites between March and October. (Note: For much of the year there is a complete ban on fires of any kind on the Pender Islands.)

By this point in your visit you are nearing the single-lane bridge that links the two islands, one-third mile (0.5 km) south of Prior Centennial park, on Canal Road.

Just before the bridge, Canal Road intersects with Aldridge Way. (Once you've been to the wooden plank bridge, you may want to return to investigate Aldridge, if only to reach the road-end site on Medicine Beach with its boat launch and views south of Bedwell Harbour.) Beside the road next to the wooden plank bridge are two rock cairns. The plaque affixed to the newer of the two, installed in 1993 by the Pender Island Museum Society, acknowledges the use of this location by local natives, primarily between 6000 and 2000 years ago. Xelisen, or helisen, is a Coast Salish word meaning "lying between," a reference to the narrow isthmus that once connected the two halves of Pender Island. Now a provincial heritage site, Xelisen was once where the original inhabitants came to harvest the abundance of food found in the rich waters and on nearby beaches.

While there is more of North Pender Island to explore, principally in the Buck and Magic lakes district (reached by travelling west of the bridge on Aldridge to Schooner Way), the flavour of the island changes here to one of a modern subdivision. In fact, it was the development of Magic Lake in the 1960s that sparked a community revolt against such drastic changes, resulting in the formation of the Islands Trust, an administrative body of elected officials from the various Gulf Islands.

Today, this area of Pender has a settled appearance, with beach access at a variety of locations. Don't let me discourage you from exploring here if you have time. There are, for example, several good bed and breakfasts on this part of the island, including the Sunnyside on Cutlass Court (629-6293), which serves up tasty Chinese food for takeout on Tuesday, Thursday and Saturday evenings.

SOUTH PENDER ISLAND   The very nature of the land changes as soon as you cross the bridge linking North and South Pender. (Although the islands were separated in 1903, the bridge wasn't built until 1955.) The north flank of Mount Norman confronts you as soon as you've made the transition, forcing travel on Canal Road around to the east: to the west the road runs only a short distance, passing the trailhead of Mount Norman Regional Park before ending near the boundary of Beaumont Provincial Marine Park. The two parks share a common boundary. From the trailhead to the top of Mount Norman is a steep 30-minute walk along an old Crown Zellerbach forest road. The mess left beside the road, a result of recent logging, is also typical of many deforested sites on southern Vancouver Island. Reforestation has not masked these ill effects. All of this notwithstanding, make an effort to climb to the top to enjoy the views if the weather is clear (if it's cloudy, leave this one for another time). Once on top, don't just settle for the viewpoint, looking north to Saltspring Island and west over Bedwell Harbour to Vancouver Island. Take the overgrown trail through the salal that begins close to the viewpoint boardwalk. In several minutes you will reach the east side of the mountain, from where you can see the weathered western flanks of Saturna Island rising from the waters of Plumper Sound. Although you can't quite make out the passage separating Mayne and Saturna islands from this vantage, you can, with the help of binoculars, look across at the mainland, with the sandy bluffs around Washington State's Birch Bay one of the more visible landmarks. If you're here on a weekday, chances are you'll be able to pinpoint Vancouver's location from the brown layer of smog hanging in the air above the city. When viewed from out here, the scale of Vancouver's current pollution problem becomes truly alarming.

Canal Road hugs the eastern side of South Pender Island for about 2.5 mi. (4 km) before merging with Spalding Road, which then leads back across the island past the old Henshaw family farm to Bedwell Harbour Island Resort, a popular place in summer but closed up tight come mid-September. The original settlement here has been consumed by fire several times and what now stands has been built to simulate a heritage appearance. If you stop here, look for a historic inscription on the rock face next to the swimming pool. Chiselled in large letters and painted silver, it reads "1905 HMS Egeria." Placed here by Captain Parry, commander of the last Royal Survey ship on Canada's west coast, the marker assisted chartmakers in keeping proper bearings. (Captain Pender, from whom the islands take their name, was one of three English navy captains, Richards and Vancouver being the other two, who followed after Captain Cook's early explorations to do detailed chartings of this area.) The open area of land next to the marker, currently carrying the euphemistic designation "Doggy Paradise," was the site of the original post office, a traditional gathering place for early island residents.

Just north of the marina at the Bedwell resort you can make out the profile of Skull Islet and, in the woods behind, the walk-in campsites of Beaumont Provincial Marine Park. It will take you 20 minutes to paddle to the park from the marina, or from Medicine Beach (mentioned earlier) on North Pender Island. There are a dozen picnic tables and campsites arranged around the beach at Beaumont, which also has a fresh-water pump and a toilet. The old-growth forest here is unlike any other on the island: well spaced, with a tall canopy of branches sheltering a grassy embankment. A loop trail runs from the beach up onto the bluffs above Bedwell Harbour. This is a thoroughly pleasant park to visit, with much more going for it in the way of natural charm than Prior Centennial park.

Spalding Road merges with Gowlland Point Road on the hillside above Bedwell Resort. By this time the road has become somewhat less crooked and twisty than up island on Canal Road, but in places it will still provide a real test for cyclists. The farther south along Gowlland you go, the more level the ground becomes, until you reach one of the prettiest, most captivating beaches on the whole of the Pender Islands. Big views open up here: northeast to Saturna Island's Monarch Head, with Mount Baker rising in the distance; southeast across Boundary Pass to the American San Juan Islands; south through a maze of channels and small islands towards Victoria and

Hurricane Ridge on the Olympic Peninsula. A big rock, prominent on the beach, displays a rainbow of colours: ferrous red streaks lend it a glazed appearance, while its unoxidized interior, visible through openings on the surface, has the look of frozen white sap from a balsam fir. Gowlland Point's pebble beach must be quite percussive during winter storms, which slam the southeast end of the island with a regularity that has residents accustomed to being without electricity for days afterwards.

If you've come this far with a car-top boat, you can launch here or back a short way off Gowlland Point Road at the foot of Craddock Road. Off Craddock Road on Southlands Drive is the rustic Whalepointe Bed and Breakfast (629-6155), boasting one of the most scenic settings of any on the islands.

32 | GABRIOLA ISLAND

Not quite nestled in Nanaimo's embrace, yet close enough to feel like it's a partner of the Harbour City, Gabriola Island is another piece in the Gulf Island jigsaw puzzle worth adding to your collection of travel memories. Although it's second largest in size and population of all the southern Gulf Islands, you won't be overwhelmed by a choice of destinations for your day trip. Gabriola's modest elevation invites you to explore on foot along the island's weathered coastline, where sandstone formations dazzle the imagination. Visit any of its three provincial parks to become enchanted by Gabriola's unique natural identity. Come with your car and boat if you wish to explore the calm waters in the shelter of the Flat Top Islands, or walk or ride your bicycle to reach the picnic grounds and beaches. Don't leave the island without first having seen the ancient rock carvings that populate an open field near Gabriola's south end.

In the late 1700s, Spanish explorers Galiano and Valdés, as well as the English navy under the command of Captain Vancouver, arrived on the northwest coast of the continent to begin some serious surveying. During the summers of 1791 and 1792 their ships simultaneously charted the waters and islands of the Strait of Georgia. (Unknown to Captain Vancouver at the time was the fact that the body of water he named the *Gulf* of Georgia was actually a strait. The misnomer stuck and some still use it today. The English sailing master also failed to identify the mouth of the mighty Fraser River, or else it would be known by a far different name.)

When it came to naming the most northerly of the southern

184

Gulf Islands, the Spanish got here first. The name Gabriola is a twisted, third-hand interpretation of the Spanish word *gaviota* (seagull), which quickly metamorphosed into Punta de Gaviola, and then to Gabriola by the mid-1850s. There's still evidence of this transition in the form of small Gaviola Island, a member of the Flat Top Islands chain, located just offshore at Gabriola's east end. Gaviola, Lily, Acorn, Tugboat and five other islands in the Flat Top chain shelter Silva Bay, site of one of the island's earliest European settlements.

During investigations of the shorelines around present-day Nanaimo and Gabriola Island, which lies 3 mi. (5 km) east of Vancouver Island in Northumberland Channel, the survey crews marvelled at various zoomorphic images—petroglyphs—carved in the bedrock. No one among the large resident population of Coast Salish Indians could explain the petroglyphs' origins. Since the Salish have a strong tradition of oral history, this would seem to date the petroglyphs back a considerable distance in time. Visiting Gabriola today, you can share in the sense of wonder, both at forms carved in sandstone by relentlessly repeated rhythms of nature—tides, winds, waves—and those etched by human hands.

Ferries to Gabriola Island from Vancouver are best caught from Horseshoe Bay rather than the Tsawwassen terminal. You'll arrive at the B.C. Ferries terminal in Nanaimo's Departure Bay in under two hours. Watch for Gabriola's white sandstone cliffs on the southern horizon as you approach Departure Bay. There is regularly scheduled bus service to downtown Nanaimo for foot passengers. Once there, it's a short five-minute walk from the Hudson's Bay Company Bastion beside the inner harbour to the Gabriola ferry dock. Gabriola is easily identified offshore to the east; closer at hand, Newcastle and Protection islands shelter Nanaimo's inner harbour.

Ferries to Gabriola leave every hour from 6:30 A.M. to 10:45 P.M. (departure times vary), at a round-trip cost of about $3 for foot passengers. Sailing time to Descanso Bay on Gabriola is 20 minutes. Pick up a complimentary island map when you purchase your ferry ticket. It will orient you upon arrival and will also help you decide which location to visit. As Gabriola is a narrow island about 12 mi. (20 km) long, how much of it you can explore over the course of a day's visit will be determined by whether you've come on foot, with a bicycle or by car.

There are three provincial parks on the island—Gabriola Sands and Sandwell at the north end, and Drumbeg on the extreme south—and one of Gabriola's most famous attractions, the naturally shaped sandstone formations known as the Malaspina Galleries, is only a short distance from the government wharf at Descanso Bay. Otherwise, there are relatively few points of public access to the beach.

Descanso Bay is a snug harbour with a wee pub, the White Hart, waiting to greet visitors. It's up to you whether you make this your first stop or last. You can confine your visit to any or all of four destinations on the northern half of the island, or do some serious travelling to four more sites on the southern half of Gabriola—a serious walk for those on foot. Unlike in the city, though, where hitchhiking has fallen into disfavour, out here on the islands it's still a possibility.

GABRIOLA SANDS PROVINCIAL PARK   It's an easy 1.2 mi. (2 km) on paved Taylor Bay Road from Descanso Bay to Gabriola Sands Provincial Park, a day-use picnic and beach area on Taylor and Pilot bays first opened in 1960. Grass fields surround the bays, lending a breezy feeling to the park. Walking out along the beach on Taylor Bay brings you past eroded sandstone formations characteristic of many Gulf Island coastlines. The Malaspina Galleries, the best known of these sandstone formations, are a short distance south of the park. The easiest approach to the Galleries is to follow Malaspina Drive, which leads west off Taylor Bay Road. Take the trail from the road's end out to the point, turn left, and scramble back along the rocks to the southern side of the point.

Archival photographs from earlier this century show the Malaspina Galleries as a smooth curl of rock in the shape of a cresting wave. Today that form is showing signs of erosion, which lends it the appearance of a chipped-tooth smile. Graffiti has been carved and painted on the walls by those who wish to leave a testament of their presence. Despite this vandalism, the smooth semicavernous gallery is still a cozy place to shelter.

Travelling up island past Gabriola Sands park, follow Berry Point Road east of Taylor and Pilot bays to reach Entrance Island Lookout and the beach at Orlebar Point near the end of the road on the northern tip of the island. You can watch the ferries chugging in and out of Departure Bay, giving Entrance Island's lighthouse a wide berth; to the north and east the open waters of the Strait of Georgia spread towards the Sunshine Coast and across to Vancouver's North Shore mountains.

SANDWELL PROVINCIAL PARK   After the Malaspina Galleries, visitors well-enough equipped to do a little scrambling around in search of a secluded beach should make the effort to find Sandwell Provincial Park. This relative newcomer on Gabriola was given official park status in 1988. To find the park, follow South Road a short distance from the ferry dock at Descanso Bay to its intersection with North Road, the commercial centre of the island. Take North Road for 2 mi. (3 km) to Barrett Road, where you make the first of a series of left turns, followed by lefts at Bluewater, Bond and finally Strand, which you trace to its end. There is public parking here. The short, steep trail to the sand and pebble beach is challenging; sturdy footwear will help. If your appetite for sandstone formations has been whetted by what you've already seen, you'll love what's in store here at Lock Bay, where it appears that a baker has been shaping dough, now miraculously transformed into rock.

GABRIOLA'S PETROGLYPHS   You'll find equally fascinating rockwork, carved by human hands, on the southern half of Gabriola on the island's west side, 6 mi. (10 km) south of Descanso Bay. As you travel along South Road on the way to the petroglyphs you'll pass Brickyard Beach, a picnic site on False Narrows that looks across at Mudge Island. This beach is where bricks from an old factory were dumped during the 1930s. Bald eagles, blue herons, harbour seals and California sea lions gather here when the herring and eulachon are running in late winter. Eagles also winter in large numbers in the Gabriola region. Watch for as many as two dozen at a time perched like ornaments on the bare branches of trees overlooking False Narrows.

South Road turns inland as it passes a magnificent viewpoint overlooking Pylades Channel. From the shore you look south at De Courcy Island to the west and Valdes Island to the east. Past here a community hall and fire station appear on the north side of the road, then the Gabriola United Church. Turn in here to find the trail to a significant petroglyph site.

The solitary examples of petroglyphs in Sandwell Provincial Park and near the government wharf at Degnen Bay on the southeastern end feature dorsal fins and flukes, which make

Ancient petroglyphs on Gabriola

these designs easily identifiable as marine life, perhaps killer whales or porpoises. They're located near the tide line, and it's quite possible they were carved as an act of invocation or propitiation. Some of the designs have an X-ray quality, showing off their interior bone structure, while others depict faces peering outward like friendly gargoyles.

Much harder to decode is the menagerie of images in the field a short distance behind the United Church. Shielded from sight by a thick coat of moss for many years, these carvings were originally unearthed by Mary and Ted Bentley and their family in 1976. Since then the Bentleys have documented their discovery in a book, *Gabriola: Petroglyph Island* (Sono Nis Press, 1981), and have worked to ensure the preservation and well-being of the site through public education.

A trail leads through the forest from the church to a flat rock outcropping the size of several city lots. Moss carpets much of the rock face, framing a host of petroglyphs that lie revealed in faint outline. Their fluid forms have been shaped by imaginations given full rein. This field is a storybook, and a creation myth or two would seem to be behind its deeply resonant theme.

Human figures are interspersed among the animal menagerie as the petroglyphs spiral gently uphill towards the forest. As you kneel beside the rocks, peering back through the frosted windowpane of time, you'll find yourself flying kite after kite of hypotheses in the breeze sweeping across the creation-filled field.

If you are visiting this site on a Sunday, take time to visit the United Church to view its exceptional collection of stained-glass windows, installed by local artist Delores Brace several years ago. The congregations of this small island church and others like it work on behalf of the homeless in Vancouver, collecting used clothing and raising money through bake sales.

SOUTH TO SILVA BAY   East of the United Church is Drumbeg Provincial Park, established in 1971 and still somewhat of a secret on Gabriola. To find your way to its secluded beach, turn right off South Road onto Coast Road, then shortly thereafter right again onto Stalker Road. Watch for the small lane leading down to the water on your left, marked by a green provincial park sign posted on a tree.

Farther still along South Road is the sheltered enclave at Silva Bay. You can easily see why Silva Bay was one of the first pieces of land on Gabriola to be settled by Europeans in the 1880s. The bay is a popular stopover for marine traffic in summer. Nearby is a log church, St. Martin's, built in 1912. Today it is shared by both Anglicans and Catholics. No matter what time of year you may be visiting, Silva Bay is always a welcome point of rest, especially for bicycle riders. It's also a good place to launch a boat to explore the nearby Flat Top Islands.

Here at Silva Bay, North and South roads converge. You can circle around Gabriola without having to retrace your way, though the views along North Road are sheltered by overhanging forest for much of the way.

BOATING ◄
CYCLING ◄
PICNICKING ◄
SWIMMING ◄
VIEWPOINTS ◄
WALKING ◄

Yes, this may be cheating a bit: Newcastle isn't really one of the Gulf islands, and Vancouver Island definitely isn't. But Nanaimo is so easy to get to by B.C. Ferry that it and Newcastle should be honorary additions to your island-hop. Visitors on a day trip can stroll from the B.C. Ferry terminal at Departure Bay to Nanaimo's inner harbour along a seawall promenade opened in 1986, or take in the natural attractions of several nearby parks. In summer months a foot-passenger ferry runs from the harbour to nearby Newcastle Island Provincial Park.

Nanaimo, or Sne-ny-mo, is said to be an Island Halkomelem word meaning "people of many names." Before the arrival of the first Europeans, several Indian communities in the Sne-ny-mo region had formed a confederation to provide better protection against raids by outsiders. Over the past century Nanaimo has become known as the Harbour City because of its naturally sheltered deep-water port. It is situated on a narrow coastal plain, surrounded by rich agricultural land and dense forests, and for a century between the 1850s and the 1950s was the centre of a large coal-mining operation.

It's also the home of the oldest preserved Hudson's Bay Company bastion in Canada. This two-storey wooden tower, completed in 1853, dominated the inner harbour as a paramilitary installation until it was turned into a museum in 1910. During summer months it now functions as a tourist information centre. A noon-gun ceremony is performed during July and August.

The city's inner streets are laid out in a radial pattern popular in England a century ago, quite distinct from the usual grid. The streets around the inner harbour may remind visitors of Vancouver's Gastown, with its cobblestone surfaces and block upon block of heritage buildings. In Nanaimo's case, the graceful curve of many of the streets lends an air of intimacy to the inner city.

One shop in particular that visitors will want to search out is the Scotch Bakery, at 87 Commercial Street where Commercial intersects with Wharf. Operated by the Wilson family since 1892, this may well be the home of the internationally reknowned Nanaimo bar, a form of chocolate fridgecake. The essential ingredients of a true Nanaimo bar are layers of chocolate and vanilla cream on a cookie base. No one seems certain of the origin of the confection, though one version of the recipe has been traced to Dutch settlers who brought the formula with them at the turn of the century.

NEWCASTLE ISLAND PROVINCIAL PARK   Newcastle Island and aptly named Protection Island perfectly shelter Nanaimo's inner harbour. The whole of Newcastle, formerly the site of coal and sandstone quarries as well as a fish-salting plant, was turned into a provincial park in 1961. Visitors can still see many signs of the former commercial activity on the island. The old sandstone quarry is fascinating for the remnants of partly completed pillars. Kids and adults will both enjoy scrambling around on their smooth shapes. (Pillars quarried here support the roof of the U.S. Federal Mint in San Francisco.)

Newcastle Island is a hub of activity in summer months, when the foot-passenger ferry sails to it from downtown Nanaimo, but the rest of the year it's a much more subdued environment. Off-season visitors make their way to the island via private water taxi service or by dint of their own efforts. For those who cross by ferry from Vancouver with a boat on top of their car, there is a launch next to the ferry terminal in Departure Bay. You can paddle from there to the government wharf on Newcastle's south end.

Newcastle Island is a bird-watcher's paradise, especially for shorebirds such as the red-billed black oystercatcher. The island is also intermeshed with trails leading off in many directions. From a variety of viewpoints you can take in the sight of the Coast Mountains in the distance across the Strait of Georgia, or

Pipers Lagoon

of the Vancouver Island Ranges rising to the north of Nanaimo. If you'd like to spend the night there are 18 walk-in campsites with wood, water and toilet facilities. The island even has room for Mallard Lake, complete with a beaver colony.

PIPERS LAGOON PARK   For day trippers on bicycles (or for car travellers leaving the ferry who aren't in a hurry to get past Nanaimo), here's a suggestion for a neat little jaunt that might well act as a warm-up for something you're planning on a much larger scale. Cycle from the ferry terminal to Pipers Lagoon, a city park with a wild side.

Chances are that if you've landed at the B.C. Ferries docks in Nanaimo's Departure Bay before you've seen Pipers Lagoon Park in the distance to the north without knowing what it was. As is so often the case, when you get to the park it is nothing like you have imagined.

To begin, perhaps you thought of the coastline north from Nanaimo to Nanoose Bay as rather flat and uninteresting. This misapprehension might have been fostered by your travels along the stretch of the Island Highway immediately beyond Nanaimo—

truly one long strip mall that is more to be endured than enjoyed.

This time, instead of following the flow of traffic from the ferry to the highway, escape on Departure Bay Road, which follows the natural arch around the north arm of Departure Bay and runs past a broad stretch of public beach and the Pacific Biological Research Station, up and down and around a few curves and through an oceanfront neighbourhood where you might like to live if you were to move to Nanaimo. From the Departure Bay ferry terminal, follow the flow of traffic uphill on Brechin Street towards the Island Highway. Just before the highway, turn right onto Departure Bay Road and right again onto Hammond Bay Road. Follow this road until a sign appears for Pipers Lagoon Park. The main parking lot is at the end of Place Road, and the boat launch is at the end of Charlaine Road. There's another small road-end access at the foot of Lagoon Road. From Departure Bay, it's an easy 3 mi. (5 km) to Pipers Lagoon Park, nestled at the foot of Sugarloaf Mountain.

At first glance, the park looks rather uncomplicated, a simple stretch of beach with a trail running off to a treed headland. Several hours later you'll realize how wrong first impressions can often be!

As you set out from the parking lot along a rough trail to explore the headland, with the open waters of Horswell Channel to the east and the sheltered calm sea of the lagoon on the leeward side, one of the first things that becomes apparent is the difference in the flora from one side to the other. Eelgrass thrives on the shore of the lagoon, while kelp beds bob in the gulf, with a profusion of wildflowers everywhere. Columbian blacktail deer frequently come out from the nearby forest to walk the curve of the lagoon, nibbling on new growth as they cast a wary eye at visitors scambling over a rocky knoll on their way to the far reaches of the headland. Now, suddenly, you have access to the series of small coves that indent this point of land. A forest made up almost exclusively of Garry oak spreads its limbs high above. In warm months the closer you look for wildflowers, the more you'll see—bring an identification guide with you. As you round a corner, a mounting wind from the gulf may blow in hard, sending you searching for shelter after a few minutes' observation of the boats being tossed around in the swells. In the distance to the south you can see ferries making their way in and out of Departure Bay. Suddenly, you seem a world away.

Cosseted in the lagoon are two small islets almost entirely taken up by old fishing shanties built cheek by jowl. Boarded up most months, these shacks are taken over each year by those in the know and used as summer squats. At low tide it's possible to wade over to them from the public boat launch located just north of the parking lot. A summer swim in the warm waters of the lagoon is ideal, just the right tonic after cycling up from the ferry.

As you rest or picnic, you may wonder if there's really any need to press on. If you've still got energy to burn, head north to nearby Lantzville for a look at a charming island town off the beaten path. Towns like this are becoming increasingly hard to find amid all the new construction that has overrun Vancouver Island's popular east coast in the past several years.

INDEX